Twayne's United States Authors Series

Sylvia E. Bowman, *Editor*

INDIANA UNIVERSITY

F. Scott Fitzgerald

F. Scott Fitzgerald

F. SCOTT FITZGERALD

By KENNETH EBLE

TWAYNE PUBLISHERS
A DIVISION OF G. K. HALL & CO., BOSTON

Library of Congress Cataloging in Publication Data

Eble, Kenneth Eugene.
   F. Scott Fitzgerald.

   (Twayne's United States authors series;
TUSAS 36)
   Bibliography: p. 169
   Includes index.
   1.   Fitzgerald, Francis Scott Key 1896-1940.
   2.   Authors, American — 20th century — Biography
PS35110.19Z6   197F1   813'.5'2   (B)   77-429
ISBN 0-8057-7183-2 (Hardcover)
ISBN 0-8057-7423-8 (Paperback)
First Paperback Edition, March 1984

To Melissa, Geoffrey, and James

Contents

About the Author

Kenneth Eble, a professor of English at the University of Utah, specializes in the humanities and American literature. He received his M. A. degree from the University of Iowa and his Ph. D. from Columbia University in 1956 with a dissertation on William Dean Howells. He has published widely on Howells and other literary subjects, and his most recent book in American literature is a collection of critical essays about F. Scott Fitzgerald, published by McGraw-Hill in 1973.

Professor Eble has had an equally distinguished career as a writer and scholar active in support of higher education. His books include *The Profane Comedy: American Higher Education in the Sixties* and *A Perfect Education*, both for Macmillan, and *Professors as Teachers* and *The Craft of Teaching* (1976), for Jossey-Bass Publishing Company. He was chairman of Committee C on Research, Teaching and Publication of the American Association of University Professors from 1970 to 1976, and Director of the *Project to Improve College Teaching* for the American Association of University Professors and the Association of American Colleges from 1969 to 1971.

Professor Eble served as chairman of the Department of English at the University of Utah from 1964 to 1969, and he was the first faculty member to be named to the position of University Professor at Utah for 1976–77. He lives with his wife and three children in Salt Lake City, Utah.

Preface

In 1963, when the first edition of this study was published, I noted that "twenty years after his death, F. Scott Fitzgerald, in his life and in his writing, is almost as fascinating to his audience as he was in the 1920's." Now, a dozen years later, Fitzgerald is still a valuable commercial as well as literary property. The movie of *The Great Gatsby* (1974), the television special, "Scott Fitzgerald in Hollywood" (1975), Sheilah Graham's *The Real F. Scott Fitzgerald* (1976) and other memoirs, and a continuing run of dissertations and scholarly articles attest to this author's durability. During this period, so many more of his works have been reprinted that very little remains that is not easily available to the general reader. Indeed, with the reproduction in 1974 of the scrapbooks and the albums of Scott and Zelda Fitzgerald (*The Romantic Egoists* edited by Matthew J. Bruccoli, Scottie Fitzgerald Smith, and Joan P. Kerr), material that was once available only to scholars became the personal property of anyone willing to pay twenty-five dollars for a handsome coffee-table book.

The mixed reaction to the lavishly produced movie version of *The Great Gatsby* may suggest a diminishing of interest in both the Fitzgerald legend and the works. In the 1960's and after, Americans may not be so preoccupied with success as they were earlier in the century. If so, fascination with Fitzgerald's sudden success may draw fewer readers to his work. Filtered through the haze of commercial exploitation of nostalgia, the 1920's may not seem so much fascinating as quaint; and Fitzgerald's fiction may seem remote, both dated and mannered, as it seriously or joyously concerns itself with that bygone era. More important, post–World-War-II fiction is not like that of writers born at the turn of the century. By now, it is obvious that Realistic, socially conscious fiction is not the type of fiction which holds the interest of serious readers today. The popularity of John Barth, Kurt Vonnegut, Thomas Pynchon, and Jerzy Kosinski does not rest on the view of either the fiction or the world that is found in Fitzgerald. For these writers, Realism no longer suffices as a means of comprehending experience, and their responses to modern life reach beyond specific criticism of American character and manners. As this century comes to an end, the Realist strain which established itself at the end of the last century is itself losing its vitality and is being replaced by different literary techniques embodying different sensibilities.

As Fitzgerald's work retains a place in American literature, I think it will be seen more and more as related to the novel of manners. What detracted from his claim to serious attention in the 1920's—that he was in his own life and in his writing the arch representative of the Jazz Age—may now be regarded as a more comprehensive interest in how people behave as social beings. The manners he describes best are not just those of New York in the gaudy 1920's, or even of an America at a crucial period when innocence was being corrupted, but the manners of those striving, whatever their time or place, for wealth or respectability, fame or love, or some idealistic fulfillment.

Fitzgerald's best work, *The Great Gatsby*, is one of literature's most successful embodiments of the Romantic response to life. "Gatsby *is* great," Robert Ornstein asserted, "because his dream, however naïve, gaudy, and unattainable, is one of the grand illusions of the race, which keep men from becoming too old or too wise or too cynical of their human limitations."[1] I do not make extravagant claims for the depth and precision of Fitzgerald's Romantic vision. He was not a Goethe, though the tightness of *Gatsby* and its central love story bear comparison with Part One of *Faust*. He was not a Keats, though few writers other than Fitzgerald have been more responsive to that poet or more moving in describing the effect of his poetry: "For a while after you quit Keats all other poetry seems to be only whistling or humming."[2] Fitzgerald comprehended the Romantic vision and created characters who lived by it, and he preserved it by the characteristic act of the Romantic—by sweating over the written word as if to preserve something from the flux of life.

Even today, readers may have difficulty in reconciling the achievement of *Gatsby* with Fitzgerald's other popular fiction. There is still a mystery about how everything came together for Fitzgerald in this favorite novel and about how it is such a great advance over *This Side of Paradise* and *The Beautiful and Damned*. The mystery may be partially explained by recognizing the magnitude of Fitzgerald's ambitions and his channeling of these ambitions into learning the craft of writing. By the time he experienced Princeton and had the chance to widen his acquaintance with other would-be writers, his ambitions had crystallized into the remark reported by Edmund Wilson, "I want to be one of the greatest writers who ever lived, don't you?"[3]

In this short book that is an introductory one, full justice cannot be done either to the author's life or to all of his fiction. The biographical account in these pages owes greatly to the other exhaustive biographical works, but the shaping, the emphasis, and the interpretation are my own. I have not attempted to alter my book because of the greater understanding we now possess of Zelda Fitzgerald and of Scott and Zelda's relationship. The question of how much Zelda was victimized by Scott is, to me, still an open question; and the facts that have come to light seem not to alter the basic one that both the Fitzgeralds were not only self-destructive but destructive of each other. I have not, therefore, felt compelled to intrude new biographical facts or insights into the basic story of either Fitzgerald's swift rise or his slow but inexorable collapse. As I wrote in 1963, "Talented as he was, his crack-up and his early death are more than mere domestic tragedy, if somewhat short of the high tragedy rarely found outside the Greek theatre or Elizabethan playhouse. Observed as he observed it, written about it as he had to write about it, fought against in the very act of observing and writing, Fitzgerald's 'high trajectory' and his agonizing descent deserve the name of tragedy."[4]

Fitzgerald's literary achievement rests on a body of work—novels, short stories, and essays—distinguished for style, craftsmanship, and honesty and strength of vision. As more and more of Fitzgerald's work has been republished, a reader has a better chance to see Fitzgerald somewhat as he must have been in the 1920's—a popular writer who turned his hand wherever the opportunity afforded and still a writer with a talent which appears in flashes in passages of individual stories and novels but which sustains itself in his best work.

The chronology at the beginning of the book furnishes an outline of biographical facts; the separate chapters follow a chronological order but keep the works in the foreground. The chapters are not separate essays about individual works but parts of a continuous narrative designed to bring out the defining characteristics of Fitzgerald's writing. Since the novels have received the greater share of critical attention, somewhat more attention has been given to the short stories. In addition to minor changes here and there in the text, my main revisions appear in this new preface and in Chapter Ten, "Final Assessment." This final chapter reflects my having read the Fitzgerald criticism that has appeared since the book's first publication in 1963 and my having incorporated my assessment of this material in it as well as in the annotated secondary bibliography.

I wish to acknowledge with thanks permission from the following publishers and publications: Houghton Mifflin Company and Arthur Mizener for material from *The Far Side of Paradise*; New Directions for material from *The Crack-Up*, copyright 1945; Charles Scribner's Sons for material from Fitzgerald's writings and from Andrew Turnbull's *Scott Fitzgerald*. A grant from the University of Utah Research Fund enabled me to consult the Fitzgerald materials at Princeton, and I acknowledge with thanks permission to use these materials granted by Alexander Clark, then Curator of Manuscripts at Princeton Library, and Mr. Ivan von Auw of Harold Ober Associates.

KENNETH E. EBLE

University of Utah

Chronology

1896   Francis Scott Key Fitzgerald born September 24, St. Paul, Minnesota.

1898–
1908   Father employed by Proctor and Gamble; family lives in Buffalo and Syracuse.

1908   Father loses job; moves back to St. Paul.

1911   September: Fitzgerald sent to Newman School, Hackensack, N. J.

1913   September: enrolls in Princeton.

1915   December: leaves Princeton because of ill health and low grades; returns to St. Paul.

1916   September: begins at Princeton again.

1917   October: leaves Princeton without a degree; receives commission as 2nd Lieutenant; November 20, leaves for Fort Leavenworth.

1918   June: transfers to Camp Sheridan, near Montgomery, Alabama. Receives news that Ginevra King is going to be married. Summer, meets Zelda Sayre, then eighteen.

1919   February 18, discharged from Army. Takes job with Barron Collier agency writing advertising copy; writes stories at night, all rejected.

1919   July: quits job and leaves for St. Paul to rewrite novel. September 16, *This Side of Paradise* accepted by Scribner's. September to December: writes and sells nine stories to *Smart Set*, *Scribner's* and the *Post*.

1920   March 26, *This Side of Paradise* published. April 3, marries Zelda Sayre in Rectory of St. Patrick's Cathedral, New York.

1921   May 3, first trip to Europe; to France and Italy, back to London by end of June; returns to Montgomery, Alabama, in July.

1921   August: rents house in St. Paul; lives there and in vicinity for fourteen months; daughter, Frances Scott Fitzgerald born October 26.

1922   March 4, *The Beautiful and Damned* published; September: *Tales of the Jazz Age*.

1922 October: moves to rented house in Great Neck, New York; lives there for twenty months unable to make ends meet.

1923 November 19, *The Vegetable* opens and closes in Atlantic City.

1923 November to April, 1924, produces eleven stories and earns $17,000. Friendship with Ring Lardner.

1924 May: second trip to Europe; lives abroad—St. Raphaël, Rome, Capri, Paris, Antibes—for next two and a half years. Meets Gerald Murphy.

1925 April 10, *The Great Gatsby* published; meets Ernest Hemingway.

1926– Fallow period, "1000 parties and no work," publishes only
1927 seven stories and two articles. Begins *The World's Fair*, a novel of matricide. Publishes "How to Waste Material," praising Ernest Hemingway.

1926 December: returns to United States.

1927 January: goes to Hollywood for first assignment writing for the movies.

1927 March: moves into Ellerslie, outside Wilmington, Delaware.

1928 Zelda Fitzgerald gets dancing obsession; summer in Paris, back to Ellerslie in September.

1929 March: begins the second long stay in Europe—Riviera. Paris, Montreux, Algeria—for almost two and a half years.

1930 April: Zelda Fitzgerald has first major breakdown; goes to clinic in Switzerland for treatment. Meets Thomas Wolfe.

1931 January: death of Fitzgerald's father.

1931 September: returns permanently to the United States; to Hollywood for Metro-Goldwyn-Mayer until January, 1932.

1931 November: death of Zelda's father.

1934 January: Zelda Fitzgerald back in sanitarium; is in and out of sanitariums through rest of Fitzgerald's life.

1934 April 12, *Tender Is the Night* published.

1935– Period of "crack-up," increasing alcoholism, physical ill-
1937 nesses; lives at Tryon, Hendersonville, and Asheville, North Carolina, and Cambridge Arms, Baltimore; Zelda in Highland Sanitarium near Asheville.

1936 September: death of Fitzgerald's mother.

1937 June: signed contract with Metro-Goldwyn-Mayer for six months at $1000 a week; option picked up for twelve additional months. Meets Sheilah Graham.

Chronology

1940   April: works briefly for United Artists; continues work on last novel, *The Last Tycoon.*

1940   November: first heart attack; December 21, second heart attack, death.

1948   March 10, Zelda Fitzgerald dies in fire at Highland Sanitarium.

CHAPTER 1

The Boy from St. Paul

I WAS Dick Whittington up from the country gaping at the trained bears," Fitzgerald wrote in 1932, describing his first impressions of New York. Throughout his life, he remained the man from the provinces, the boy from St. Paul, Minnesota. His sense of fundamental decencies, his bedazzlement at wealth and power, his sensitivity to snubs and slights, even his need for the right romantic affection from the supremely right romantic girl, could only mean so much and persist so long in a provincial. What marks him is that he so often made what was common, banal, and transient into something singular, fresh, and enduring.

Though the Fitzgerald family moved to Buffalo in 1898, when Scott was two, and did not return until 1908, St. Paul is as fittingly his home as Montgomery, Alabama, was Zelda Sayre's. In "The Ice Palace," the best of his early stories, he captured the essential characteristics of the Northern and Southern cities superbly. Many other stories—"Winter Dreams," "Absolution," and those in the Basil Lee group—drew upon Fitzgerald's adolescence and early manhood in the Midwest. *The Great Gatsby* succeeds in being more than it seems at first reading partly because of the effectiveness of the larger contrast between the American West and East.

I *Family Background*

By 1908, St. Paul was a city of close to 200,000. Its two foremost citizens were James J. Hill, the builder of the Great Northern Railroad, and Archbishop John Ireland, the builder of the great Catholic diocese for which St. Paul's Cathedral was begun in 1906 and dedicated in 1915. The man of power and the priest inhabited Fitzgerald's being all of his life. In addition, St. Paul was a city in which hereditary position meant much.

Once past the frontier stage, St. Paul became conservative, aristocratic, smug. For all that, it accommodated itself to commercial wealth, and the best families soon included the wealthiest families. Almost all guide books speak of the air of superiority with which St. Paul faces Minneapolis and of the fact that "the sons and grandsons of the sound merchant and banking class, still give their stamp to the community."[1]

Fitzgerald's mother's family belonged to this sound merchant class. What security he enjoyed in his youth was of a shaky sort and came from the wealth amassed by his grandfather, P. F. McQuillan, before the turn of the century. When he died in 1877, Grandfather McQuillan left a million-dollar wholesale grocery business and a personal fortune of over $250,000. The newspaper obituary paid him this tribute:

> He came here a poor boy with but a few dollars in his pocket, depending solely on a clear head, sound judgment, good habits, strict honesty, and willing hands, with strict integrity his guiding motive. How these qualities have aided him is shown in the immense business he has built up, the acquisition of large property outside, and the universal respect felt for him by the business men of the country.

The family fortune was ample to support his mother's two spinster sisters and to give solid backing to her two brothers and herself. When Scott and Zelda settled on the Riviera, they were repeating a trip his parents had made on their honeymoon. Before her marriage, his mother had visited Europe four times with the McQuillan family. When Grandmother McQuillan died in 1913, Fitzgerald's family's share from the estate reached $125,000. As late as 1936, when his mother died, the residue from the estate was $42,000.

Fitzgerald's "Scrapbook" gives evidence of the family's position in St. Paul. The plays which he wrote and played in received extensive coverage in the society pages of the daily newspaper. Later, his activities at Princeton were given similar attention, not only because he was a local boy making good in an Eastern school, but because he was the son of "Mr. and Mrs. Edward Fitzgerald, broker, 589 Summit Avenue"—and the grandson of P. F. McQuillan. Summit Avenue was the street which "epitomized St. Paul's golden day." There the McQuillan mansion stood, and in various houses in the vicinity Fitzgerald spent his youth. "In a house below the average on a street above the average"—so Fitzgerald describes one of the houses in which he lived in his teens.

In a haunting way, the McQuillan fortune and his own father's failure, his parents' hopes and aspirations and their personal tragedies prefigure Fitzgerald's life and work. His ancestry was not merely that of other Midwestern provincial writers. He was, as Midwestern urban society goes, "somebody," and he moved naturally into the country club set that defines society in the smaller American cities.

The wealth and prestige of his mother's family, however, was balanced against his father's inability to support a family by his own efforts. In practical terms, this may have meant the pre-occupation peculiar to families living solely on limited inherited wealth: keeping the principal intact. It meant the postures of affluence constantly bowing to the necessities for economy. It meant grave family conferences when Scott was to be sent to Newman School in New Jersey and later to Princeton. There is little evidence that he suffered want at either place. There is some basis for conjecturing that his wanton spending when he found the money coming in goes back to his family's economic situation. The shadowy principal was always there making all other financial transactions less than ultimate, even less than crucial. The family fortune gave him the right and the predis-position to live grandly if he could; it gave him the license to spend whatever came in by his own efforts; it gave him the compulsion to spend in defiance of the economies that shabby gentility had forced upon his youth. "I enclose $1.00," his father wrote to Master Scott Fitzgerald in July, 1909. "Spend it liberally, generously, carefully, judiciously, sensibly. Get from it pleasure, wisdom, health and experience."[2]

Fitzgerald's sense of tragedy may also have developed out of his parents' past. Their life, observed by a sensitive boy, conveyed its share of pain. Both came to marriage late: he was thirty-seven, she was thirty. Their first two children died a short time before Fitzgerald was born; a subsequent child died in infancy. By the time Fitzgerald had reached the keenly sensitive years of adolescence, both parents were past fifty: the father, a man who couldn't hold a job, who dwelt in the past, and on some image of himself superior to the one he was able to maintain; the mother, a woman of odd appearance and manner whose thwarted affections found some release in a sentimental devotion to her only son. Not until later was Fitzgerald able to see the true pathos of lives beginning late and slowly running down. After his mother's death, when he was going through the many small treasures of the past she had saved, he wrote: "When I saw all this it turned me inside out realizing how unhappy her temperament made her and how she clung to the end to all things that would remind her of moments of snatched happiness."[3]

Because of the wealth of his mother's family, because of that family's deeper roots in St. Paul, because of his mother's excessive and somewhat eccentric devotion, and because of the pallid character of his father, Fitzgerald's youth was dominated by his mother and by her family. His later attitudes are mixed— the novel he began work on and stuck to for a number of years after 1925 was a story of matricide—but the family and the social world which he was privileged to circulate among became a solid part of his fiction. His father seldom appears; indeed, in the Basil Duke Lee stories, he is already dead when Basil is introduced.

Yet, despite the dominant position of his mother, Fitzgerald's deepest mature feelings are not toward her family—"straight potato-famine Irish" he once called them. It is rather the Maryland ancestors of his father, with their distant kinship with Francis Scott Key, that exercised the greatest fascination. The treasured image is that of his father, the Southern gentleman who can trace his ancestry back to the colonies and the Revolution and who should have possessed wealth as he possessed manners: as a natural gift unaffected by falling sales or declining energies. In a moving passage in the manuscript "The Death of My Father," written in 1931, Fitzgerald said, "I loved my father— always deep in my subconscious I have referred judgments back to him, [to] what he would have thought or done."[4]

II *Boyhood and Adolescence*

Very little of Scott Fitzgerald's life in Buffalo and Syracuse before the family moved back to St. Paul gets into his fiction. When it does, it is in such minor ways as placing Dick Diver's childhood home in Buffalo and having him drift off into upper New York State at the end of *Tender is the Night*. Fitzgerald's later account of these years in his "Ledger" mentions the birth of his sister Annabel, the only other Fitzgerald child to survive childhood; visits back to St. Paul, to his paternal aunt's home in Maryland, and to Atlantic City; and various changes of residence. He tells about crying when he was sent to school in 1900 (his parents took him out after one morning), about telling "enormous lies to older people," about running away at six, about a birthday party to which no one came. At nine, "he fell under the spell of a Catholic preacher, Father Fallon of the Church of the Holy Angels."

The details of these years reveal a somewhat pampered and sheltered boy, an occupant of apartments and rented houses, an inheritor of a sense of family superiority without much visible evidence to support it. As they appear in the "Ledger," these years seem almost as rich in experience as the later years in St. Paul; the experiences of 1907 in Buffalo shade off into those of St. Paul in the next year. Though the years were neither idyllic nor wretched, they were marked by impermanence and instability.

The details of Fitzgerald's life in St. Paul from 1908 to 1922 are quickly told. At St. Paul Academy, he published his first story in 1909 in *Now and Then,* the school magazine. His life during his two years there is full of evidences of accumulating feelings which were to be expended on the writing of two decades. Among these experiences were a succession of athletic attempts in which he—shorter and lighter than the other boys—performed bravely but poorly; a number of clubs for which he was usually organizer and leader; a "Thoughtbook," the earliest of his account books of his activities and emotions; attendance at a dancing class which heightened his sensitivity toward social position; and a considerable amount of juvenile writing, particularly of plays for which he was often writer, producer, and actor.[5]

In 1911, he began a period of two years at Newman Academy, a Catholic boarding school in Hackensack, New Jersey. Newman gave him his first chance to visit New York, and the plays he saw there helped to keep his literary ambitions closely tied to the stage throughout this early period. During the summers and vacations in St. Paul, he fell in love. One memorable summer, he directed "The Captured Shadow," a play written by fifteen-year-old F. Scott Fitzgerald. He also played the lead, that of a suave gentleman burglar, apparently one of Fitzgerald's youthful ideals.

Girls—his thoughts of them and of what they were thinking of him—filled his mind in these adolescent years. His crushes were many. The most enduring, its memory lasting his entire life, was over Ginevra King, a Chicago girl who enjoyed the wealth and social position to which Fitzgerald was always drawn. He met her in St. Paul in January, 1915, on the next to the last day of Christmas vacation, and he continued the romance in person and through an ardent correspondence. By the time ill health and low grades forced him to withdraw from Princeton at the end of 1915, the romance was on the wane. "No news from Ginevra," is entered in his "Ledger" in August. The nine months he spent at home until he could enter Princeton again in the fall term of 1916 were among the emptiest of his life. It was plain then that Ginevra, like Minnie Bibble of his stories, had looked over his shoulder to fall in love with someone else.

Through these years and the half-dozen to follow, St. Paul was a place to return to from the various defeats and distractions of a wider world. He spent the summer of 1917, as usual, in St. Paul; in July he was examined at Fort Snelling for a provisional appointment as a second lieutenant in the regular army. Though he began the fall term at Princeton, he withdrew in October and was inducted into the army at Fort Leavenworth, Kansas, the next month. When he came back to St. Paul again, it was a return from defeat with a resolve to gather his forces for another assault. The war was over, his first novel had been rejected, his engagement with Zelda Sayre was broken off, his stories had been sent back, his career in advertising had foundered at $90.00 a month. "I retired," Fitzgerald wrote later, "not on my profits, but on my liabilities, and crept home to St. Paul to 'finish a novel'."[6]

It was from St. Paul that he mailed the manuscript to Scribner's, and it was there that he received the news of acceptance. The St. Paul paper announced his success in terms even the young Fitzgerald could not have improved upon: "He is a young man less than 24 years old, but in spite of his youth he has written a serious book of more than 100,000 words, which has gained the recognition of the big New York publishing concern."[7]

Though from this time on Fitzgerald's fiction and his life are bound up with his "incalculable city" of New York, the publication of his novel did not quite close out his life in St. Paul. When he returned for an extended period—from August, 1921 until October, 1922—it was again a return to a haven after the disordered life of New York City and the suburbs during the Fitzgeralds' first year of marriage. The reasons for returning were obvious: Fitzgerald needed a place to work and his wife a place to have their child. When they left St. Paul for New York a year after their daughter (their only child) was born, they did not again return. The boy from St. Paul had accepted his uneasy place in the world.

III *The Basil Duke Lee Stories*

The factual details of these years, and more important, the emotional facts of this early experience, appear in a dozen or more stories—some written close upon the experience, others long after. It is to these stories that we now turn to consider what of this youthful experience was important to Fitzgerald's writing. The stories which most clearly and connectedly explore his youth are the nine Basil Duke Lee stories, eight of which appeared in the *Saturday Evening Post* from April, 1928, to April, 1929. Five were collected in *Taps at Reveille*, three others in Arthur Mizener's *Afternoon of an Author*.

The stories are as excellent in craftsmanship as any stories Fitzgerald ever wrote. They are all the more remarkable for having been written during the first period at Ellerslie and the frantic summer of 1928 abroad, a time in which Fitzgerald's growing inability to control himself and Zelda Fitzgerald's developing schizophrenia must have made steady work very difficult. The stories are evidence of Fitzgerald's meticulous attention to dates and events and of his ability to evoke the precise shades of feeling that accompanied events of the past. The dates during which the stories take place—the earliest in 1909 while Basil is still attending Mrs. Cary's Academy, the last in the fall he enrolls at Yale—tally exactly with Fitzgerald's life from his last year in Buffalo to his enrollment at Princeton. White Bear Lake, where Fitzgerald spent part of his summers (he was a member of the White Bear Lake Yacht Club), becomes Black Bear Lake; "The Captured Shadow," the play Fitzgerald wrote and produced in 1912, is the same play Basil writes and produces the same year; the note in Fitzgerald's "Ledger," September, 1911, "Attended State Fair and took children on rollercoaster," refers to the same fair that Basil attends the same fall; even the small size of Newman Academy (actually only sixty pupils) is used in the Basil story in which St. Regis loses valiantly to Exeter: "good for a school of only 158."[8]

But more important than the fact that the fictional details fit the actuality of Fitzgerald's experience is that these stories, written as they were at the peak of Fitzgerald's skill, are able to capture with precision the emotions and attitudes of Fitzgerald's youth. Fitzgerald had not, as Basil vowed he would, become president at twenty five; but he had become almost as famous. He had fulfilled his dreams and had proved the practicality of dreaming large. And yet through all the stories and all the dreams of success runs the theme of desires not quite satisfied, of last-minute rescues from shame and despair, of the "worst things" as later recorded in his Notebook: "To be in bed and sleep not, / To want for one who comes not, / To try to please and please not."[9]

"That Kind of Party" (unpublished), "The Scandal Detectives," and "A Night at the Fair"—the three stories set earliest in time—are all about Basil Duke Lee's life before he leaves for boarding school. Basil is described as "rather small as yet, bright and lazy at school . . . by occupation actor, athlete, scholar, philatelist and collector of cigar bands." All these stories convey the atmosphere, as Fitzgerald described it, of adolescence at a time when Basil and his generation "were sitting with disarming quiet upon the still unhatched eggs of the mid-twentieth century." All three turn upon Basil's relations with girls; and all three have the pattern, familiar in all of Fitzgerald's work, of a young man swinging back and forth between humiliation and success.

The first of the stories, "That Kind of Party," was rejected by the *Saturday Evening Post* because, according to Arthur Mizener, "its editors did not care to believe that children of ten and eleven played kissing games." The story was published in the Fitzgerald number of the *Princeton University Library Chronicle* (Summer, 1951). In the typescript, Fitzgerald had changed the names of the characters, but the situation and feeling are clearly those of the Basil Duke Lee stories. Though it is not clear when the story was written, it clearly falls at the beginning of the series, for the setting in time is 1909. Basil (called Terence R. Tipton in the manuscript) and his friends are ten and eleven years old. A good many, perhaps most, of the details are from the years in Buffalo and Syracuse. References to Tonawanda, to relatives upstate, to apartment-house living, and to Mrs. Cary's Academy were drawn from the Fitzgeralds' life before they moved back to St. Paul.

The story is a weak story; it depends too much on trickery, and the author does not yet see the central character clearly. Terence uses all his cunning to try to arrange a party in which kissing games will be the sole entertainment. Despite all his pains, his plans are discovered, and he escapes complete humiliation at the end only because Dolly Bartlett, the girl he's been after, has been sufficiently impressed with his daring to ask him for dinner. Thus the story ends with the hero displaying an attitude which is present throughout the series: "It was time things went better. In one day he had committed insolence and forgery and assaulted both the crippled and the blind. His punishment obviously was to be in this life. But for the moment it did not seem important—anything might happen in one blessed hour."

In "The Scandal Detectives," Basil attempts to scare rival Hubert Blair by sending him anonymous threats and by planning to waylay him and put him in a garbage can. To get Hubert out of his house after dark, Basil disguises his voice as that of Imogene Bissell and invites him to a party. The plan miscarries, partly because the timing goes wrong but, more important, because Basil develops scruples at the last moment. Confronting Hubert, Basil, in disguise, "for a moment felt morally alone." After he lets Hubert escape, the desperadoes—Basil, Riply Buckner, and Bill Kampf—invite themselves to Imogene's supposed party claiming that they too had been deceived. While the Bissells and Mr. Blair puzzle over the uproarious laughter of the three boys, they goad Hubert into enlarging fantastically upon his desperate encounter. In the end, Hubert goes to the seashore leaving Basil some of his dazzling mannerisms and a brief moment of romantic pain in recognizing that what another girl has said is probably true: "Hubert Blair is the nicest boy in town and you're the most conceited."

Light as it is, "The Scandal Detectives" is an interesting story for the concern with values which runs through it. "The Book of Scandal" in the story (Fitzgerald's "Thoughtbook") was not composed for the purpose of gaining power. Rather it was treasured against the time when adverse fortune might strike, when the subject of one of its entries might wish "to do something to Basil and Riply." The threats made against Hubert are not really carried out; in fact, they miscarry in a comic way. The triumph Basil achieves is one of the imagination, the most common kind of victory Fitzgerald permits his youthful heroes. The real spoils—the whispering, scuffling, and kissing with Imogene Bissell—have gone to Hubert.

Similarly, in "A Night at the Fair," Basil uses his head to gain another qualified triumph—this time over the humiliation of being the only boy still condemned to wear short pants. The girls this time are pick-ups; the successful pursuers are a fast older boy, Elwood Leaming, Riply Buckner, and Hubert Blair. Basil's moral scruples are as delicate in this story as in the former one. When he finds himself with a girl that he cannot endure, his instinctive decency will not let himself hurt her openly, but it cannot prevent him from finding a means of escape. When Hubert Blair, calling himself Bill Jones, takes Riply's girl away, Basil slips off leaving his date with Riply. Later, sitting safely in the grandstand beside Gladys Van Schellinger, a girl both rich and proper, Basil watches Elwood, Riply, Hubert, and the girls pass by in a sort of "Lilliputian burlesque of the wild gay life." Basil's position at that moment is both morally and imaginatively superior and, for that reason, intensely satisfying. He lets himself enjoy Riply's shame for a moment—"the natural cruelty of his species toward the doomed was not yet disguised by hypocrisy"—but a moment later he suggests to Riply's aunt, in that tone by which he was almost always able to please adults, that it would be a sort of mistake to tell Riply's mother. When Gladys moves toward Basil, "her breath warm on his cheek . . . that vague unexciting quality about her more than compensated for by her exquisite delicacy," she says, "Basil—Basil, when you come tomorrow, will you bring that Hubert Blair?"

With "The Freshest Boy," the scene shifts to Basil at St. Regis. Chronologically, the story moves forward only a few months. Emotionally, it moves a good way. Technically, even the minor characters are sharply etched. The opening scene of Part Four, which reveals the character of the football coach, Mr. Rooney, could not be improved upon. The whole story makes a meaningful contrast between the Basil who fits easily into the St. Paul adolescent crowd and the Basil who arrives at St. Regis to become the most unpopular boy in the school.

The story does more than evoke a momentary nostalgia for one's youth. To some degree, each of these stories separates itself from the conventional story of childhood or adolescence by strongly suggesting the connection between this time and the time to come. Booth Tarkington's Penrod or Owen Johnson's Lawrenceville boys can hardly be imagined out of either the setting or the time in which they are placed. Basil Lee can. The ending of "The Freshest Boy," though overly dramatic, is explicit in suggesting this continuity, but all of the stories have this sense of connection somewhere within them.

"The Freshest Boy" takes itself more seriously as a story than

the earlier ones; it ends seriously rather than comically. Basil
has more moments of insight. He sees the necessity for understanding his own unpopularity at the same time that he is
trying to understand a wider range of behavior in the person
of Mr. Rooney and in the conversation between the radiant girl
and Ted Fay, the Yale football captain. Out of this last, Basil
gathers "that life for everybody was a struggle, sometimes magnificent from a distance, but always difficult and surprisingly
simple and a little sad."

"The Freshest Boy" is the central story in the Basil group in
that the Midwestern boy of the first three is now brought into
the larger world for which he has yearned and is sharply
rebuffed by that world. He carries that experience with him into
the next three stories as the vital part of his past. The preparation and departure for Yale mark a change of climate for which
all that has passed is background.

"He Thinks He's Wonderful" moves ahead to the end of
Basil's first year at St. Regis. Basil's aspirations tally almost
precisely with Fitzgerald's: "He wanted to be a great writer,
a great athlete, popular, romantic, brilliant, and always happy."
(When the story was revised for inclusion in *Taps at Reveille*,
Fitzgerald left out both "a great writer" and "romantic.") The
story uses another event of Fitzgerald's life—his exclusion from
a dance in St. Paul—to dramatize the turning of Fortune's wheel.
In the story, the dance is preceded by a game of Truth and
Consequences in which Basil is named the favorite of three of
the girls. Despite what he has learned from being "the freshest
boy" at St. Regis, he cannot disguise his satisfaction over this
evidence of his charm. Offered the chance of making a new
friend with a boy who is not yet on to him, Basil throws it away
by setting out to tell the boy how to be as popular as he is.
How well Fitzgerald reveals his youthful character becomes
apparent when one compares this episode with the lengthy in-
structions Fitzgerald gave to his sister Annabel during his first
year at Princeton, reprinted at length in Andrew Turnbull's
biography.[10] Though Basil manages to beg his way to the dance,
he bores Imogene when he gets there and discovers he's been left
out again, this time from a trip being planned by the others.

The second half of the story introduces the most engaging
woman in these stories, with the most engaging name in Fitzgerald's fiction: Erminie Gilberte Labouisse Bibble.[11] A New
Orleans girl, she is in St. Paul because her parents are trying to

see if outdoor life will take her mind off indoor pleasures. Only girls like Minnie can sense at a glance the essential Basil. Once again, however, Basil's moment of glory is brief. In another excellent comic scene, Basil rides a few miles with Minnie's father and talks away his chances of being invited to tour Glacier National Park with the family. "Imagine having to listen to that fresh kid for two weeks," says Mr. Bibble. Basil's horrified realization that "he had undone the behavior of three days in half an hour," was the kind of lesson learned too late that Fitzgerald must have tormented himself with in the years before this story was written. At the end, Basil gets at least second best. He gets to drive his grandfather's electric, and he is last seen driving Imogene away at a speed somewhat in excess of what he told her mother it would go.

"The Captured Shadow" is the account of the production of Fitzgerald's play of the same name in St. Paul in the summer of 1912. Some of the difficulties Basil has in getting the play on the boards are probably fictional, but the general account and the specific feelings are undoubtedly very close to the real experience. Here, Basil's imagination finds its way into art. His St. Regis past still clings to him—Hubert Blair quits the show because of Basil's "bossiness"—but the play is a success in all respects. Yet that success is not allowed to stand without a touch of foreboding. The story ends with Basil's mother leaning over him as he sleeps, "God, help him! help him," she prayed, "because he needs help that I can't give him any more."

In the next story, one short year after being "Bossy" Lee at St. Regis, Basil becomes his school's hero in a football game with Exeter. (The factual counterpart was Newman's victory over Kingsley, October 26, 1912, in which Fitzgerald, substituting for the injured captain, distinguished himself for his "snap and bang.") Basil plays so brilliantly that a St. Regis alumnus, John Granby, now at Princeton, singles him out as the man to redeem youth through setting a perfect example. This is the starting point for "The Perfect Life," a story which shows how much Fitzgerald can make of a "plot" story. Basil succumbs completely, though briefly, to the missionary charm of Granby. He gives up tobacco, liquor, women, and a host of sins of which he is only dimly aware. Basil's earlier dreams are subtly deflated in the ironic way Fitzgerald treats Basil's quest for the perfect life. The paragraph in which Basil defines his aspirations is worth quoting in full:

To be of great wit and conversational powers, and simultaneously strong and serious and silent. To be generous and open and self-sacrificing, yet to be somewhat mysterious and sensitive and even a little bitter with melancholy. To be both light and dark. To harmonize this, to melt all this down into a single man—ah, there was something to be done. The very thought of such perfection crystallized his vitality into an ecstasy of ambition. For a moment longer his soul followed the speeding lights toward the metropolis; then resolutely he arose, put out his cigarette on the window sill, and turning on his reading lamp, began to note down a set of requirements for the perfect life.

The rest of the story concerns itself with Basil's introduction to Jobena Dorsey, a typical Fitzgerald girl who has sinned little but has the appearance of having sinned greatly. Basil tries to get her to go with him into the perfect life, but he only succeeds in driving her to consider eloping with a sentimental wastrel named Skiddy De Vinci. How Basil prevents the elopement is the final joke in a conspicuously clever plot. Basil goes back to his less-than-perfect life, and Jobena finds him infinitely more interesting when he does.

The last two stories are concerned with Basil's life at the time of his departure for Yale. "Forging Ahead" is the most undisguised wish-fulfillment story in the group. Its details, such as his employment in the Great Northern Railroad car shops and the untappable wealth of his mother's family, are taken directly from Fitzgerald's last adolescent summer in St. Paul. Basil has grown somewhat older, but he is still dependent upon his imagination and a kindly fate for what triumphs he gains. Two visions are foremost: "the faraway East, that he had loved with a vast nostaglia since he had first read books about great cities," and "the inevitable, incomparable girl."

Yale, which Fitzgerald whimsically chose instead of Princeton, represents the East; Minnie Bibble is the girl, as she is in "Basil and Cleopatra," the last of the series. In this story, Basil, like so many of Fitzgerald's heroes, is in love with love. His wooing is complicated by the necessity of inducing in the girl the right response, not only to him but to love as well. The details of "Forging Ahead" are too complicated to elaborate. It is chiefly concerned with Basil's plan to attend Yale in the fall and the threat to those plans which arises from financial losses suffered by his immediate family. He is forced to work, then to seek help from his great-uncle at the price of becoming the steady escort for the uncle's plain daughter, Rhoda Sinclair. All this complicates his pursuit of Minnie. In the end, Minnie, Yale, his family pride, his bright future, are all secured by the sudden sale of a block of family property for $400,000.

"Basil and Cleopatra" brings the series to a close. It does so, Arthur Mizener concludes, because Basil, now on the verge of manhood, is forced to recognize with grief and regret that "you couldn't be with women incessantly." Since the stories were written in 1928, there is a more obvious reason for its ending the series: the stories which followed Basil into Yale and after had already been written. Basil leaves off where Amory Blaine of *This Side of Paradise* begins. The fine passage with which "Basil and Cleopatra" ends is very close to a similar passage in *This Side of Paradise*:

> Jubal the impossible came up with an air of possession, and Basil's heart went bobbing off around the ballroom in a pink silk dress. Lost again in a fog of indecision, he walked out on the veranda. There was a flurry of premature snow in the air and the stars looked cold. Staring up at them he saw that they were his stars as always—symbols of ambition, struggle and glory. The wind blew through them, trumpeting that high white note for which he always listened, and the thin-blown clouds, stripped for battle, passed in review. The scene was of an unparalleled brightness and magnificence, and only the practiced eye of the commander saw that one star was no longer there.

A comparison with the other passage, written ten years earlier, shows how Fitzgerald developed as a writer over these first ten years:

> No more to wait the twilight of the moon in this sequestered vale of star and spire, for one eternal morning of desire passes to time and earthy afternoon. Here, Heraclitus, did you find in fire and shifting things the prophecy you hurled down the dead years; this midnight my desire will see, shadowed among the embers, furled in flame, the splendor and the sadness of the world.[12]

Romantic longing inspired both passages; only in the first has he developed the style which captures the feelings convincingly.

The story "Basil and Cleopatra" is one in which fulfillment and disappointment, the comic and the serious, the real and the imagined, are neatly and effectively balanced. The irony throughout is deft. Basil finds out that Erminie has not merely passed him over for his football rival, Littleboy Le Moyne, but has already passed Le Moyne over for "a sad bird named Jubal." Le Moyne, less wary than Basil, saves him from making a fool of himself over a lost cause. Basil passes up the invitation to succumb to Cleopatra once more, but not without the regret that goes with leaving the immortal woman "who wore her sins like stars."

Throughout the story, Fitzgerald's preoccupation with the truth (and the falsity) of the romantic vision gives the story a substantiality beyond its rather thin plot. Basil as a man of destiny, an idea playfully treated in all the stories of this series, is here treated with some depth. His destiny, in turn, is involved in that Faustian desire for the moment of satisfaction. It is Fitzgerald's singular ability to dignify the trivial while remaining faintly ironic toward it that gives this story its best effects. Thus, the football game is treated as the counterpart of Antony's conquests of empire, and Fitzgerald's authorial reflections stand out as quite superior to the context: "Like most Americans, he was seldom able really to grasp the moment, to say: 'This, for me, is the great equation by which everything else will be measured; this is the golden time,' but for once the present was sufficient. He was going to spend two hours in a country where life ran at the pace he demanded of it."

The highly developed technique in all these stories may be suggested by a number of observations about this one. First, the irony in "Basil and Cleopatra" makes the comparison with Antony and Cleopatra more than a mere use of an obvious parallel. The closing paragraph, in its imagery as in its explicit meaning, creates the heightened feelings of the classical story even as it illuminates the untragic romance being described. The foreshadowing in the second paragraph is as effective in this way as it is felicitous in its phrasing: "He was almost unconscious that they stood in a railroad station and entirely unconscious that she had just glanced over his shoulder and fallen in love with another young man." Second, the ordering of events and use of events is precisely right. The movement from the Southern city, to New Haven, to the Yale football field puts the world of dalliance against the world of conquest. And, after the conquest, the temptation that always reaches out to the victor provides the final drama of the story. Finally, the characters: Erminie, Littleboy Le Moyne, Jobena Dorsey, and Basil are used with more fullness than in other stories. Basil still is mortgaged to the past even as he is steadily pulled into the future, but his

awareness of what is happening and his judgment of it have
increased greatly.

IV   *"Absolution"* and *"Winter Dreams"*

The Basil Duke Lee stories are consistently the best of the
stories dealing with Fitzgerald's early youth. Among a number
of stories written earlier, "Absolution" (1922) and "Winter
Dreams" (1924) make the most imaginative and effective use of
this same past. "Absolution," one of Fitzgerald's most admired
stories, succeeds despite its flaws. No story of Fitzgerald's so
suggests the "literary" short story of the early 1920's. The weep-
ing priest, the wheat terrible to look upon, the ineffectual yet
tyrannical father, the sensitive young boy for whom "the pressure
of his environment had driven him into the lonely secret road of
adolescence," all bring to mind *Winesburg, Ohio* and a multitude
of similar stories of throbbing souls in the simmering Midwest.
The heavy hand of heredity and the brooding presence of environment make this story the most "naturalistic" story Fitzgerald
ever wrote.

The boy of eleven in "Absolution," Rudolph Miller, is not an
earlier version of Basil Duke Lee, though one could guess that
religion, guilt, and shame were a part of Basil's (and Fitzgerald's)
past that does not come through in the Basil stories. The father
is not Basil's father nor is he Fitzgerald's. The setting is certainly
manufactured for the occasion, and it is weak in being that
vaguely foreboding Midwest which many writers before and
during Fitzgerald's time used for background. Even though the
incidents upon which the story turns—the telling of a lie in the
confessional and the father's striking the son—were occurrences
in Fitzgerald's life, they are used in the story to dramatize the
fictional relationship between father, son, and mad priest.

Nevertheless, the story fits in with the Basil Duke Lee stories
and *The Great Gatsby*. The story was written, Fitzgerald said,
as a beginning for *Gatsby*, but close readers of that novel will
recognize that only superficial resemblances tie Rudolph Miller
and James Gatz together. What the character shares with Gatsby
is also shared with Basil Lee, Nick Carraway of *The Great Gatsby*,
and Dick Diver of *Tender Is the Night*, whose pasts cling to
them but whose lives shape themselves year by year in accord-
ance with some Platonic image of themselves. In Rudolph Miller,
however, this shaping force is hardly apparent, and we are glad

that Fitzgerald did not incorporate this background into *The Great Gatsby* and by so doing risk making the novel just another story which sentimentalizes over the adverse effects of a barren youth.

"Winter Dreams" begins with the experiences of another fourteen-year-old boy, who is in many respects like Basil Duke Lee. Dexter Green lives in the world of his dreams and yet is shrewdly aware of his relationship to the world outside. He quits his caddying job abruptly, "unconsciously dictated to by his winter dreams" which take the tangible form of a girl of incomparable worth. Judy Jones, the girl in this story, becomes a woman who "simply made men conscious to the highest degree of her physical loveliness."

The rest of the story is a full but compressed story of the provincial boy from the middle class rising into sufficient wealth and power to claim the rich girl of his dreams. It was, as Fitzgerald said, a short version of *The Great Gatsby,* and its central character interests us not merely for his success but for the illusions that drive him to success and for "the mysterious denials and prohibitions in which life indulges." Dexter has his brief love affair with Judy Jones—of one month's duration—but in the end, as in *The Great Gatsby,* he cannot have her. "So," the story puts it, "he tasted the deep pain that is reserved for the strong, just as he had tasted for a little while the deep happiness."

The ending of the story is ironic, as Fitzgerald's ambitious stories almost always are—in part as a resort to a device of plot to which his short fiction seems committed, in part as a turning to his essential feeling for the flow of life. Dexter succeeds in Wall Street, "so well that there were no barriers too high for him." At thirty-two, he has settled in the East and has become so identified with it that a business acquaintance is surprised to learn the facts of his past: "I thought men like you were probably born and raised on Wall Street." Through this acquaintance, Dexter learns of Judy's unhappy marriage. Worse, he realizes from a casual remark of this near-stranger that she is no longer beautiful. Dexter's tears, when they come, are not for a lost love, nor even because this beauty, all beauty, fades, but for himself, and for the country of illusion, of youth, of the richness and promise of life, where his winter dreams had flourished.

The story owes much to the love affair between Fitzgerald and Ginevra King; but, as always in Fitzgerald's best work, it is not the details of real experience which give his fiction its stamp of quality, it is the essential truth evoked by the re-shaping of that experience. The worth of these stories which so closely parallel his own youth is the value that Fitzgerald draws out of every passing moment of experience. Fitzgerald's vision is clear on this point. The stories escape being merely sentimental or nostalgic because he does not rest content with re-creating a static, though memorable, past. He insists on having his past merge into present and for both to absorb the future. Unlike the characters he is most fond of describing, he can, in the act of writing, grasp the moment for his reader and make the reader realize, if only fleetingly, that "this, for me, is the golden time." Even as he writes, however, the golden time is receding into the past and the mind is already creating another time that lies ahead. So it was for Basil Duke Lee and so it is, were we capable of either admitting it or describing it, for us all.

All this Fitzgerald was learning in these early years in St. Paul. His literary apprenticeship goes back to those years not so much in what he was writing, but in what he was feeling. Though the Basil Duke Lee stories were written fifteen years after the events, they expose to our view the essential emotional past out of which Fitzgerald was to create his best work.

CHAPTER 2

Princeton

THE FIRST CHAPTER of *This Side of Paradise* provides a background for Amory Blaine before he enters Princeton. Though some events and emotions at Newman (called St. Regis in the novel) get into the book, Fitzgerald's life at Princeton and a good deal of the writing he did there furnish most of the substance. At the time Fitzgerald began to write seriously, Princeton was the one great event of his life; his romance with Ginevra King, which both brightened and darkened his last year at Princeton, was the other.

"Amory, Son of Beatrice," the first chapter, is interesting not only because it was Fitzgerald's first ambitious attempt to make literary use of his past, but because it furnished the suggestions for further elaborations of this material. The Basil stories just discussed were written, it should be remembered, in 1927 and 1928. *This Side of Paradise* was put into final form in 1919; the later stories appear in brief form in the novel, just as they appear in even briefer form in Fitzgerald's "Ledger." "The Freshest Boy," "He Thinks He's Wonderful," "The Perfect Life"—all are suggested in this first chapter.

Amory resembles Basil in numerous ways. His reputation at school for idling, unreliability, and superficial cleverness; his ability to ingratiate himself with adults; his easy drift into fabrication; his posturing; his triumphs and despairs; his conscience; his code; his freshness; and his dreams of becoming rather than being—all these are traits shared by the two characters. His weaknesses as Fitzgerald sees them—extreme sensitivity, vanity, self-suspicion, and lack of courage and perseverance—are also shared traits.

The most striking difference, and even this is not so different beneath the surface, is in the fictional background he gives to his two heroes' families. At twenty-two, the sense of shame

Fitzgerald seems to have felt for his family was a great deal more important to him than it was to be at thirty. Basil's father is dead before the stories are told; what we see of Basil's mother is the rather conventional maternal woman who murmurs over him at the end of "The Captured Shadow." Amory's father is left shadowy, but he is explicitly "an ineffectual, inarticulate man with a taste for Byron and a habit of drowsing over the *Encyclopaedia Britannica*," who inherits sufficient wealth to devote himself to "taking care of" Beatrice. Beatrice, Amory's mother, makes up for the pallor of the father. She may be, in part, a figure created out of Fitzgerald's annoyance with his mother's eccentricities. More than that, she creates the romantic background that Fitzgerald's own youth so lacked. Though she is, like the father in "Absolution," created to fit or explain the protagonist, she is also created out of the feelings and aspirations, unsifted as yet and only partially experienced, that went into Fitzgerald's beautiful young girls. She is any one of a number of Fitzgerald girls bringing up a boy who will in turn be swept away by someone like her. Only the irony that Fitzgerald was able to maintain in the early chapters and which was lost in many of the later ones keeps Beatrice from being unbearable.

Though Beatrice provides Amory with the kind of romantic background which life had not provided Fitzgerald, the details mix Fitzgerald's desires with the actualities of his family's past. Beatrice's fabulous wealth, her education at a convent in Rome, her absorption of an international culture, are all exaggerations, but exaggerations out of his mother's life as Mary McQuillan. Amory's transient education results from his mother's restlessness which from his fourth to his tenth year took the form of *doing* the country in his father's private car. Fitzgerald's early education was similarly transient, but his mother's restlessness took the form of moving from Buffalo to Syracuse and back to Buffalo and from house to house in between times. Beatrice's talk of Eton and Christ Church for Amory must have been akin to Mrs. Fitzgerald's ambitious desires for her son; St. Regis, the preparatory school Amory does attend, is as much Fitzgerald's school, Newman, as Amory's Princeton is Fitzgerald's Princeton.

The point of those comparisons is that Fitzgerald, in this first chapter of *This Side of Paradise*, is not so much exploring the past to find out honestly what was there as he is using the past and changing it to fit the self-image of Amory Blaine as a personage at Princeton. Fitzgerald's irony is at its best in these early chapters. The self-revelations are not embarrassingly immature as they often are in a first novel, but are vivified by style and by the flashes of perception with which Fitzgerald sees the characters. Amory's being "on to" Beatrice in the first chapter is also Fitzgerald's being "on to" Amory through at least the early parts of the book.

I *Fitzgerald at Princeton*

With "Spires and Gargoyles," Chapter Two of *This Side of Paradise,* Fitzgerald turns to his Princeton experiences. Fitzgerald enrolled in Princeton in the fall of 1913. His credentials were not sufficient to get him admitted outright (his Newman grades included an "E" in Caesar, "D" in Vergil, "C" in Cicero, and "D" and "B" in Latin grammar and composition), but he was accepted after a personal interview with the admissions officers. According to Arthur Mizener, he "was a small boy (five feet seven), slight and slope-shouldered in build, almost girlishly handsome, with yellow hair and long-lashed green eyes which seemed, because of the clearness of their whites, to stare at people with a disconcerting sharpness and curiosity."[1]

The differences and similarities between Fitzgerald and Amory are revealing. Amory is just under six feet, exceptionally but not conventionally handsome. He has a young face, penetrating eyes, and lacks the intense animal magnetism that so often accompanies beauty in men or women. "I didn't have the two top things: great animal magnetism or money," Fitzgerald later wrote in his notebooks. "I had the two second things, though: good looks and intelligence. So I always got the top girl."[2] Christian Gauss, writing about these years when he was a member of the Princeton faculty, described Fitzgerald's classic profile, and he added: "Inwardly he was anything but Greek and often reminded me of Dostoyevski's *The Brothers Karamazov* for there were in him oddly uncoordinated elements of all three of the brothers, including the gentle and saintly Aliosha."[3]

Princeton, during the years Fitzgerald attended, was going through what Dean Gauss called "the Indian Summer of the 'College Customs' era." Compulsory chapel ended in 1915; the Triangle Club's traveling shows played as far west as St. Louis, St. Paul, and Chicago; the *Nassau Lit,* at the bottom in prestige in 1906 to 1911, passed through "five of its most fruitful and successful years" from 1912 to 1917. Fitzgerald's life at Princeton reflects precisely the split between the "college customs" spirit and the serious interest in literature and learning. The two sides can be seen in the contrast between Amory Blaine's first two years at Princeton and his last two, but they are also apparent in Fitzgerald's actual experience and evident later in the essay about Princeton which he wrote for *College Humor* in 1927.

The romantic undergraduate Princeton is the one which materializes out of a view from afar. "Two tall spires and then suddenly all around you spreads out the loveliest riot of Gothic architecture in America, battlement linked on to battlement, hall to hall, arch-broken, vine-covered—luxuriant and lovely," is the way Fitzgerald described it in the essay. The same romantic view appears early in the novel, in Amory's characterization of Princeton as "lazy and good-looking and aristocratic," and in the entire "Spires and Gargoyles" chapter. This vision of Princeton was made up of football and the upper-class clubs; of romantic alumni like Aaron Burr, Philip Freneau and, more recently, Booth Tarkington; of classmates whose fathers controlled vast wealth and power.

There is no intellectual tradition for Fitzgerald to admire in this view of Princeton, no moral tradition. Princeton is, like Harvard and Yale, a setting for stories like Owen Johnson's *Stover at Yale,* from which Fitzgerald and countless others learned of the glories of college life. "Sam White decides me for Princeton," Fitzgerald wrote in his Scrapbook under a ticket stub for a game November 4, 1911, in which White had starred. Seeing the Princeton Glee Club in 1908 and reading Owen Johnson's essay on the clubs at Princeton about the same time were among the other experiences which inclined him toward Princeton.

The Princeton of Fitzgerald's literary interests did not appear to him until he returned in the fall of 1916. The Princeton he now saw all around him reflects his changed attitude as well as changes which were taking place on the campus. That change is described in Chapter Four, Book One, of *This Side of Paradise,* which begins: "During Amory's last two years there, while he saw it change and broaden and live up to its Gothic beauty by better means than night parades, certain individuals arrived who stirred it to its plethoric depths."[4] Fitzgerald was being precise when he wrote of Amory Blaine at the beginning of his two years at St. Regis: "for the next four years the best of Amory's intellect was concentrated on matters of popularity, the intricacies of a university social system and American Society as represented by Biltmore Teas and Hot Springs golf-links." Those four years took him through the first two years at Princeton; his last two years turned to more serious concerns. The last year-and-a-half Fitzgerald spent at Princeton led directly to the remark he made to Edmund Wilson shortly after college: "I want to be one of the greatest writers who have ever lived, don't you?"[5] During these years, he gained a wide acquaintance with late nineteenth-century poetry; read extensively such modern British authors as Shaw, Wells, and Compton Mackenzie; and developed aspirations well beyond the confines of Princeton. He also gained, in the process and after, a healthy disrespect for much that was identified with his alma mater—not a trivial gain from a college education.

Fitzgerald's academic accomplishments at Princeton were about those of Amory. He was, from the beginning, a poor student in the classroom, for he was busy at almost everything else but his studies. Though he resented all his life the imputation that he had flunked out, his record at Princeton offers little in the way of a defense. Early in his first term, he was called in because of low grades; at mid-year he had failed three subjects, had the lowest pass mark in three others, and had managed to get by in English. His average was 5.17 on a grading system in which 5 was the lowest passing mark; by June he had raised it to 4.97. From that time on he was never out of academic difficulties though he managed average grades in English and just below average in philosophy. When he returned to Princeton after dropping out in 1915-16, he did somewhat better work, getting 2's in English and French and a 3 in another course in English.[6]

His record of cuts offers a partial explanation of his grades: eighteen the first term, thirty-one the next, fifty (the maximum permitted) the next. Under the circumstances, his protest against the requirements at Princeton show more sensitivity than sense. But beneath the protests is recognition that the American college, then and now, is made rigid by course hours and credits at the same time that it encourages the students to disregard them—indeed, to disregard all intellectual life. Fitzgerald shirked his responsibilities in the usual way. His work during the first year on the *Tiger* and on the Triangle show was not precisely uneducational, but it was not academic. The pleasures of club life and of not attending class were equally unacademic. "Disgraceful," he wrote under his third term report, "but happy."

Of his many diversions, one at least was both imaginative and intellectual. This was his acquaintance with Sigourney Fay, a converted Catholic father whom Fitzgerald had met at Newman. Father Fay appears as Father Darcy in *This Side of Paradise* (the book is dedicated to Father Fay), and the nature of their discourse and of his influence upon Fitzgerald is fully suggested in the novel. Indeed, the Eleanor episode of the novel was not Fitzgerald's but a story told to him by Father Fay. Their talks were many; probably the majority of them were, like those in the novel, concerned with literature or with the exploration of the young man's developing personality. But for Father Fay, Fitzgerald's first years might have been a good deal further removed from intellectual life than glorious undergraduate Princeton already made it. Father Fay remained a close friend of Fitzgerald's until his early death at forty-three in January, 1919. Before Fitzgerald enlisted, Father Fay had proposed to take him abroad as part of a complicated mission from American Catholics to the Pope.

At the end of his freshman year, Fitzgerald returned to St. Paul for the summer and wrote, produced, and directed another play. He spent much time at the White Bear Yacht Club, but evidently did enough extra academic work to remove the conditions with which he had finished the year. He was readmitted as a sophomore in 1914, but was not permitted to take an official part in the Triangle Club. Unofficially, he went to work on the Triangle show, *his* show since he was chiefly responsible for the book and lyrics of "Fie! Fie! Fi-Fi!" which was produced during the Christmas vacation of 1914. Fitzgerald was ineligible to tour with the show, and the end of his sophomore year found him in St. Paul again, one of the more impressive Eastern college boys home for the summer. His meeting with Ginevra King six months later was both a sporting spectacle and love at first sight. She became the "lost girl," almost as ubiquitous a character in his fiction as the "lost boy" in Thomas Wolfe's. Between January, 1915, and January, 1917, when the affair broke off, Fitzgerald received sufficient letters from Ginevra to make 227 typed pages in the volume in which he later had them bound.

At the end of his sophomore year, he was invited into Cottage Club, recognized—along with Ivy, Tiger Inn, and Cap and

Gown—as one of the "big" clubs at Princeton. By now, he was one of the "big" men, secretary of the Triangle, on the editorial board of the *Tiger,* and surrounded by young men of proper breeding, poise, and charm. The soft sweet college life which such honors made possible was even more disastrous to his academic work than the distractions of freshman year had been. His cuts were more frequent—he describes a long excursion on the Jersey Coast in *This Side of Paradise*—his failures more serious, and his tendency to play the big man, "running it out" as it was called then, too often evident.

He left Princeton at the end of his sophomore year much as he had left his freshman year. The promise was more glowing; the chance of failure more threatening. That summer's activity (1915) gave him the material for "The Diamond as Big as the Ritz"; the visit to his friend Charles "Sap" Donohue's ranch was his first extended visit away from St. Paul during the summer. The trip west may indicate a lessening of genuine concern or an increasing sense of being able to "luck out" of his academic difficulties. At any rate, he did not remove previous conditions that summer and though he was readmitted, he was barred from all extracurricular activities in his junior year, 1915-16. "A year of terrible disappointments & the end of all college dreams," he later wrote in his Ledger. "Everything bad in it was my own fault." Among his other disappointments was his being ineligible to play in the Triangle show after his forthcoming appearance in it had been given extensive publicity in the St. Paul newspaper. In response, perhaps, he attended a fraternity dance in St. Paul during the Christmas holiday dressed as a stunning blonde. But before that in November, an attack of what was probably malaria put him in the infirmary and led to his withdrawal from Princeton because of illness and low grades.

The Princeton failure was one of a number of experiences which helped create the pattern to be found in Fitzgerald's fiction: success coming out of abysmal failure, or failure following hard upon success. We have already mentioned similar events in Fitzgerald's family past and the dramatization of them and others in the Basil Duke Lee stories. His leaving Princeton was the great shock, but it was also, in a way, mere confirmation of what life had already been hinting at and which was to be reconfirmed in the years following the great success of his first novel. If ever a man felt he was on Fortune's wheel, it was Fitzgerald.

II *The Romantic Egotist*

When he re-enrolled at Princeton in September, 1916, he had only faint hopes that the wheel was ascending. However it moved, the war was waiting to claim him, and his last year was marked by the feeling that college did not really matter. On the Princeton campus, feelings aroused by the war may have pushed many undergraduates to a more serious consideration of the lives they were leading. The memorable event of this academic year was the reform movement to abolish the Princeton clubs. Henry Strater (Burne Holiday in *This Side of Paradise*) led the movement. Fitzgerald's reaction to him, as it comes to us through the novel, was that of discovering new directions:

> But that night Amory was struck by Burne's intense earnestness, a quality he was accustomed to associate only with the dread stupidity, and by the great enthusiasm that struck dead chords in his heart. Burne stood vaguely for a land Amory hoped he was drifting toward—and it was almost time that land was in sight.

Strater helped Fitzgerald examine his literary enthusiasms; instead of Fitzgerald's own orthodox and dilettantish affection for Chesterton and Wells, there was a deep spiritual and material strength somehow connected with the reading of Tolstoi, Edward Carpenter, and Walt Whitman. Visiting Edmund Wilson in the apartment he now occupied in New York or going to New York with Monsignor Fay, Fitzgerald could say that "the New York of undergraduate dissipation had become a horror and though I returned to it, alas, through many an alcoholic mist, I felt each time a betrayal of a persistent idealism."[7]

These various influences toward an idealistic seriousness had their greatest consequence in intensifying his reading and in his beginning to take his writing seriously. The Victorian poets were the first of his early interests to be swept aside. His enthusiasm for Booth Tarkington, Compton Mackenzie, Shaw, Wells, and Butler overcame judgment for a time; but before long only Shaw and Wells continued to claim his attention.[8] Somewhat later, if we accept Amory's testimony, he was "puzzled and depressed" by *A Portrait of the Artist as a Young Man*; and he discovered, through Mencken, *Vandover and the Brute*, *The Damnation of Theron Ware*, and *Jennie Gerhardt*. His writing—poems, reviews, short stories—began to appear in quantity in the *Nassau Lit*; his favorite subject was Ginevra King and their burnt-out romance. Among his best friends were John Peale Bishop (Tom D'Invilliers of *This Side of Paradise*) and John Biggs, both editors of the *Lit*. A visit to Bishop's home in the summer of 1917 resulted in his first sale, a poem which *Poet Lore* bought but did not publish. "I sent twelve poems to magazines yesterday," he wrote to Edmund Wilson in September, 1917. "If I get them all back I'm going to give up poetry and turn to prose."[9]

When Fitzgerald left Princeton in the spring of 1917, he was conscious that it was the end of his college career. He remained a loyal alumnus of Princeton, after a falling-out occasioned by the publication of *This Side of Paradise*, until his death. (He was reading a copy of the alumni magazine when he suffered his fatal heart attack.) His return to Princeton for the senior year 1917-18 was only a waiting period until his commission into the army came through. He had taken the examinations that summer; his orders to report to Fort Leavenworth arrived in November, 1917. When he departed, he took with him the rough manuscript of the novel which was to become *This Side of Paradise*.

Five chapters of that novel, *The Romantic Egotist*, are in the Fitzgerald collection at Princeton. These unpublished chapters of the first novel make less of an attempt to create a convincing fictional character than to write a first-person account of Fitzgerald's life at Newman and Princeton. The immediate fictional influence may have been James Joyce's *Portrait of the Artist as a Young Man*, in addition to those authors Fitzgerald had so admired as an undergraduate. The narrator is Stephen Palms, "a loiterer on the border-land of genius," who is writing his history from his present position as a cadet in Aviation School during World War I. The first two chapters are about Newman; Chapters Three and Four are missing; and Chapter Five is a less successful version of the "Spires and Gargoyles" chapter in *This Side of Paradise*. The other extant chapters are Twelve, a version of the Eleanor episode, and Fourteen, "The Devil," a more elaborate and spookier account of the same material under the same subhead in the novel.

Judging from the partial evidence of these chapters, many of the faults, much of the material, and a large measure of the vitality remained from the earliest version to the published novel. When Fitzgerald looked back on the first version, having revised the novel thoroughly in the summer of 1919, he called it a "disconnected casserole." Though most of the young egotist's experiences were retained in the published novel, Fitzgerald compressed the experiences at Newman, elaborated those at Princeton, and tried to emphasize the continuity in the development of Amory Blaine. The style is improved in the successive versions, though the manuscripts offer little evidence of the meticulous revisions to be found in Fitzgerald's later works. Charles Donohue, Fitzgerald's close friend since his Newman days, read three installments of *The Romantic Egotist* in the fall of 1918 and was disappointed in the way the material was handled. There were too many incidents left undeveloped, too many characters sketchily portrayed; too often the humorous incidents weren't humorous nor the serious ones convincingly serious.

These faults are still evident in *This Side of Paradise*. It is a good bad book, not so much a novel as, to use Fitzgerald's own description, "a somewhat edited history of me and my imagination."[10] Or, as he referred to it later, "A Romance and a Reading List" (he paired it with *"The Sun Also Rises*: A Romance and a Guide Book"). Still later (1938) he wrote to Maxwell Perkins, ". . . looking it over, I think it is now one of the funniest books since 'Dorian Gray' in its utter spuriousness—and then, here and there, I find a page that is real and living."[11]

III   *This Side of Paradise*

A half-century after its first printing, its fakeries forgiven, its obvious connections with popular novelists of the time acknowledged—"traces of Tarkington, Chesterton, Chambers, Wells, Benson (Robert Hugh), Rupert Brooke"—and its misspellings corrected, *This Side of Paradise* offends less. Though it is still not a novel that can stand solely on its merits, it offers a good deal to the understanding of Fitzgerald as a writer.

What should not be forgotten about *This Side of Paradise* is that it is the first published version of Fitzgerald's favorite story and theme. Amory Blaine called this "definite type of biographical novel" a "quest" book. He went on:

> In the "quest" book the hero set off in life armed with the best weapons and avowedly intending to use them as such weapons are usually used, to push their possessors ahead as selfishly and blindly as possible, but the heroes of the "quest" books discovered that there might be a more magnificent use

for them. "None Other Gods," "Sinister Street," and "The Research Magnificent" [novels by Robert Hugh Benson, Compton Mackenzie, and H. G. Wells] were examples of such books; it was the latter of these three that gripped Burne Holiday and made him wonder in the beginning of senior year how much it was worth-while being a diplomatic autocrat around his club on Prospect Avenue and basking in the high lights of class office (125-26).

Fitzgerald's innocent is one more version of a common American type. Unlike Hemingway's Nick Adams, his awareness is not directed toward recognizing an abstract evil but toward understanding the distinctions which mark one man, one portion of society, off from another. His knowing of self is not an appreciation of his or mankind's metaphysical nature but of his social nature. When Amory goes off into reform and theoretical socialism, a reader should not be surprised or disappointed. The development is consistent with the character of Amory as it is created in the book. Thus considered, the philosophizing and the loose references to past history, literature, and contemporary thought may be passages we skip through, but they are proper to the book. Amory receives an education—a good one in spite of college, he argues at the end—and it is precisely that education, in "manners" in its large sense, that helps make Fitzgerald an important novelist.

The story, despite its quest motif, does not really go anyplace; Amory is not so much going someplace as going through experience. The quality of these experiences is not very high, nor are they always effectively presented; they are not particularly fresh; neither are they profoundly moving. They are, given the material, engaging and diverse enough to catch interest, and they are described with a certain freshness and frankness of detail. But what should we expect from a boy such as Amory, whose reading at the beginning of his eighteenth year was, to quote *This Side of Paradise*, " 'The Gentleman from Indiana,' 'The New Arabian Nights,' 'The Morals of Marcus Ordeyne,' 'The Man Who Was Thursday,' which he liked without understanding; 'Stover at Yale,' that became somewhat of a textbook; 'Dombey and Son,' because he thought he really should read better stuff; Robert Chambers, David Graham Phillips, and E. Phillips Oppenheim complete, and a scattering of Tennyson and Kipling" (36).

How primarily *This Side of Paradise* is Amory's book can be argued from the large proportion of the book devoted to his miscellaneous experiences. The love stories occupy less than a third of the narrative, and despite the intensity with which each is urged, they too are only passing experiences, like the others, which make their impress upon Amory's developing self. The Isabelle–Amory episode, the first love story, is the story of Ginevra and Scott's meeting transferred from its first telling in the *Nassau Lit* to the early part of the novel. The Clara episode was created out of Fitzgerald's fondness for a favorite relative, Cecelia Taylor, a first cousin on his father's side, sixteen years older than Fitzgerald and a widow with four children in 1917. The Rosalind story is once again Ginevra with a large mixture of his just-experienced love for Zelda Sayre. The Eleanor episode is a close retelling of a story told him by Father Fay.

None of these stories diverts the author's attention away from Amory. They are vignettes designed to display Amory, just as the episodes of Dick Humbird's death, the girl in the New Jersey hotel, and the appearance of the devil in the New York apartment are designed to reflect Amory. Amory the romantic egotist moves, as he should, through a hall of mirrors which display the facets of his developing personality. "In fact," Fitzgerald wrote about *The Romantic Egotist*, "woman and mirrors were preponderent [*sic*] on all the important pages." At the end of the novel, we are impressed not so much with what we can say of his personality but with the way we have felt the experiences he has gone through.

A good many of the experiences, of course, we can neither see nor feel. As Arthur Mizener has pointed out, Fitzgerald's "habit was to vamp passages of generalization here and there in a story and round it off with a piece of popular philosophizing. . . ."[12] In *This Side of Paradise*, he tends to display, often sharply, a scene and then vamp to the next one. A roughly chronological order holds the scenes together, but there is little close attention to juxtaposing scenes for effectiveness or of building from scene to scene toward a climax. He was writing the discursive novel, the loosely constructed narrative that H. G. Wells defended in 1911 as the dominant form of the modern novel.

For the most part, the first half of the book where Fitzgerald was drawing directly upon experiences, yet experiences which have had a little time to cool, is better than the last half where he is more concerned with describing states of mind which have not yet clarified in his own life. Amory's arrival at Princeton, the young men he meets, the romance with Isabelle, the outing at Asbury Park, and even the death of Dick Humbird may be regarded as mere sharp notations of the college scene; but they are sharp and both convincing and interesting. Perhaps the book begins to stagger where Amory himself did: his failing the make-up examination which ended his chances for a conventional success at Princeton.

For the next twenty pages or so, until Chapter Four of Book One begins, the narrative drags. Amory's self-analysis is too much a typical undergraduate preoccupation with finding the "real" self. It carries little conviction even though it is followed by a longer and somewhat better examination of Amory's character by Monsignor Darcy. The rest of the section is padding—Tanaduke Wylie, the futurist poet; the Devil scene; the appearance of Dick Humbird's face—and is neither very relevant to the novel nor of great interest in itself.

Though the novel is divided into two books, the real division comes at Chapter Four of Book One, almost fifty pages before Book Two begins. The change in the junior class, dramatized through Burne Holiday's change from autocrat to reformer, establishes at once the more serious direction Amory's development is to take. The conversations become heavy with ideas, less convincing, and a good deal less amusing. Of the Clara episode, the main interruption in Amory's Princeton dialogues, it can be said that her superior goodness is consistent with the new idealism now infecting Amory. Though the conversation is again artificial, Clara has her moments of perception, as when she says, "You're a slave, a bound helpless slave to one thing in the world, your imagination." After the Clara episode, the first part of the novel drifts off into a number of romantic effusions. "The voices of freshman year" surge around Tom and Amory, and as "the last light fades and drifts across the land," Amory's Princeton years come to an end.

The "Interlude" which separates the Princeton years from Amory's experiences after the war was Fitzgerald's way of excluding everything but bare mention of Amory's war experiences. The devices he used—a long letter from Monsignor Darcy; a poem "Embarking at Night," and a letter from Amory in Brest to Tom D'Invilliers at Camp Gordon, Georgia—are adequate to the need. Considering what Fitzgerald was later to make of his

tame but emotionally stirring period in the army, it is curious
that the exclusion here is so complete. Perhaps it was because
the army experience did not or could not be made to put
Amory so squarely at the center. It may also be because Fitzgerald, like most romantics, tended to endow experience with
maximum emotion long *after* the event and *after* the romantic
imagination had had time to color and intensify the experience.

Book Two of the novel is really the story of Rosalind and
Amory; the material which comes after is something of an
appendix to the whole book. (The Eleanor episode provides
a bit of unintentionally comic relief from the tedium of socio-
economic discussion.) Rosalind is the first of the Fitzgerald
girls who are to be found in numerous stories of these early
years. She is, in many ways, Amory Blaine's alter ego:

> She wants what she wants when she wants it and she is prone to
> make every one around her pretty miserable when she doesn't
> get it—but in the true sense she is not spoiled. Her fresh
> enthusiasm, her will to grow and learn, her endless faith in
> the inexhaustibility of romance, her courage and fundamental
> honesty—these things are not spoiled (174).

She refuses to marry Amory for much the same reason that
Amory himself could not be content without fame, fortune,
and the girl. Fitzgerald must have drawn heavily on Zelda
Sayre's refusals when he wrote the last part of the dialogue:

> AMORY: Are you going to marry Dawson Ryder?
> ROSALIND: Oh, don't ask me. You know I'm old in some ways—
> in others—well, I'm just a little girl. I like sunshine and pretty
> things and cheerfulness—and I dread responsibility. I don't want
> to think about pots and kitchens and brooms. I want to worry
> whether my legs will get slick and brown when I swim in the
> summer (199).

The Rosalind episode ends in the romantic sigh: " 'Oh, Amory,
what have I done to you?' (And deep under the aching sadness
that will pass in time, Rosalind feels that she has lost something,
she knows not what, she knows not why.)"[13]

The scattered events of Chapter Two, Book Two, come directly
out of Fitzgerald's experiences in the spring of 1919. After a
long drunk, Amory quits the advertising agency, sells a story
about his father's funeral, reads enormously, and begins to lose

his former literary enthusiasms.. The rest of the book concentrates on Amory's losses—heroes, women, the idea of progress, and religion—and, on his attempts to find something to believe in. "Amory was alone," the author reflects. "He had escaped from a small enclosure into a great labyrinth. He was where Goethe was when he began 'Faust'; he was where Conrad was when he wrote 'Almayer's Folly.'" The passage is not so important for Amory's grandiose comparisons as it is for the evidence it gives of Fitzgerald's high literary aspirations and of his early admiration for Conrad.

Amory's appearance as a social thinker at the end of the book is probably due to the influence Shaw and Wells still were exerting upon Fitzgerald. What it lacks is the sense of irony which Fitzgerald was able to maintain in the earlier sections of this novel and in all of his best work later on. The debate over socialism with the father of Jesse Ferrenby, a Princeton classmate who was killed in the war, is synthetic in the argument as in the contrivance which brings Amory and the elder Ferrenby together. Despite the weakness of that scene, the very last reflections of Amory as he stands along the New Jersey roadside are perceptive in substance and extremely well phrased. They are the kind of paragraphs Fitzgerald was always able to do well and with great economy in his later work. The last fully developed paragraph turns properly to the towers and spires of Princeton and to the images of the "past brooding over a new generation." The lines, "a new generation grown up to find all Gods dead, all wars fought, all faiths in man shaken," have been more widely quoted than any single passage from Fitzgerald's works.[14]

The whole last section, "Out of the Fire, Out of the Little Room," is important for what it suggests, through Amory's final analysis of himself, about Fitzgerald's temperamental affinities. Nature, he observes, can be "a rather coarse phenomenon"; "nature represented by skies and waters and far horizons was more likable." Selfishness is accepted as "the most living part" of Amory, and yet he sees that it is through "somehow transcending rather than by avoiding that selfishness that I can bring poise and balance into my life." "The problem of evil had solidified for Amory into the problem of sex." With it, "inseparably linked," was beauty. We will look more closely at this attitude in considering Fitzgerald's dramatization of evil lurking in beauty in *The Great Gatsby*. With these perceptions,

Amory concludes that "he was leaving behind him his chance of being a certain type of artist. It seemed so much more important to be a certain sort of man." Finally, the many passages about Catholicism in *This Side of Paradise*—the only Fitzgerald novel in which they are to be found—are concluded with Amory's recognition that, "for the present," acceptance of the Church of Rome was impossible. This, too, seems to represent Fitzgerald's definite and permanent separation from the Church.[15]

IV   The Importance of This Side of Paradise

The defects in *This Side of Paradise* should not blind the reader to its importance in Fitzgerald's career. It marked his movement, clumsy and pasted together as the novel often is, from a clever short-story writer and would-be poet to an ambitious novelist. All his life he was to think of himself as primarily a novelist, to save his best work for his novels, to plunder his published short stories for usable material for them. If he achieved nothing else in this first novel, he had at least taken his scattered literary effusions and his undescribed experiences, sifted them, shaped and reshaped them, often looked at them ironically, and fashioned them into a sustained narrative. Compared with the material he took directly from his *Nassau Lit* stories, the writing had improved greatly. In many rewritten passages, *This Side of Paradise* shows Fitzgerald moving to that freshness of language which became his identifying mark.

The novel took the bold step that Fitzgerald needed: it confirmed his ideas about the importance of his feelings and about his ability to put them down. It helped Fitzgerald thrash out those "ideas still in riot" that he attributes to Amory at the close of the book: his ideas about love and women, about the Church, about his past, about the importance of *being* as contrasted with *doing*. Though it borrowed heavily from the many writers to whom he was attracted, the book still has Fitzgerald's own stamp: the naïveté and honesty that is part of "the stamp that goes into my books so that people can read it blind like Braille." If Amory is not as honest with himself as Fitzgerald's later characters can be, it is chiefly from a lack of perception rather than from a deliberate desire to deceive.

Finally, though Fitzgerald placed his twin hopes of money and the girl in the book's great success, the book is not merely contrived to achieve these aims. The badness in it is not that of the professional who shrewdly calculates his effects; it is that of the ambitious amateur writer who produces what seems to him to be witty, fresh, and powerful prose. It is a much better book than *The Romantic Egotist,* the version he finished before he left Princeton. For Fitzgerald at twenty-three, it was the book he wanted to write, the book he could write, and the book that did get written. Before it even reached its audience, Fitzgerald had found his craft.

CHAPTER 3

Early Success

TO ALL young aspiring writers, Fitzgerald's success cannot help but be appealing; it came so fast and from such despair. The long-range effects of his quick and early success will be debated as long as Fitzgerald remains an important writer. The immediate effects are clear: it gave him the things his romantic self most desired—fame, money, and the girl.

In a year's time, between February 18, 1919, when he was discharged from the army, and the next year, he moved from an amateur writer whose sole publication had been in college magazines to a professional with one novel ready for publication and a dozen stories published or accepted. From the time he sold his first story, "Babes in the Woods," to *Smart Set* for $30.00, to the next year, he had made over $3,000 from magazine fiction and $2,500 from the movie rights to one of the stories. By the end of the 1920, he had made over $19,000. No wonder he could write in "How to Live on $36,000 a Year," "my income had a way of doubling every month. . . . At the end of the year it must reach half a million."

Short of finding money in the street (and this seldom happens) or winning huge sums at cards or in the market (and both require capital), writing is the most startling way to rise from poverty to fortune, from obscurity to fame. Nothing less can explain the persistence with which young men and women of widely varying talents and for little over-all return choose to flood the mails with manuscripts. Access to a typewriter and a dollar's worth of paper and stamps is the price of setting up a literary business and sending forth the products like notes in a bottle. No author has described this typical situation—and the untypical results—better than Fitzgerald did in 1937 in an essay called "Early Success."[1]

"Seventeen years ago this month I quit work or, if you

prefer, I retired from business," the essay begins. "I was through—let the Street Railway Advertising Company carry along under its own power." Fitzgerald had come back from the army to New York, planning "to trail murderers by day and do short stories by night." The newspapers didn't want him, and he became a copy writer for the Barron Collier Advertising Company at $90.00 a month. Between March and June, he wrote nineteen stories and collected, according to his own testimony, 122 rejection slips. When he did finally sell a story—to *Smart Set* in June for $30.00—the sale was not very exciting. "The real blight," he wrote, "was that my story had been written in college two years before, and a dozen new ones hadn't even drawn a personal letter. The implication was that I was on the down-grade at twenty-two. I spent the thirty dollars on a magenta feather fan for a girl in Alabama."

The girl was Zelda Sayre; with the thought of her growing "nervous" in Montgomery disturbing his nights, and the job at the agency ruining his days, he despaired of the one and chucked the other and "crept home to St. Paul to 'finish a novel.'" "That novel, begun in a training camp late in the war, was my ace in the hole. I had put it aside when I got a job in New York, but I was as constantly aware of it as of the shoe with cardboard in the sole, during all one desolate spring. It was like the fox and goose and the bag of beans. If I stopped working to finish the novel, I lost the girl."

Elsewhere in the same essay, he describes his feelings: "I was in love with a whirlwind and I must spin a net big enough to catch it out of my head, a head full of trickling nickels and sliding dimes, the incessant music box of the poor."

And then, suddenly, with "that first wild wind of success," everything changed. The period between Fitzgerald's deepest despair (in "May Day," the story created out of this period, Fitzgerald's fictional self commits suicide) and the beginnings of his success, was a little over three months. With the acceptance of the novel, the metamorphosis of amateur into professional began. Events and people began to be situations and characters for stories. The confidence of the professional began to appear in his work. "The Ice Palace," written during this first flush of success, is one of his best stories; "The Camel's Back," a very competent story, was written in twenty-two consecutive hours.

Equally important, the continuing acceptances meant that the other prize—Zelda Sayre—was now within reach. His wooing became a kind of courtship by financial statement, a flurry of letters and telegrams conveying who had bought what and for how much. "All in three days," he wrote, "I got married and the presses were pounding out *This Side of Paradise* like they pound out extras in the movies." The book and the girl were the center of that short and precious time. The effects, as Fitzgerald carefully considered them twenty years later, were these:

> The dream had been early realized and the realization carried with it a certain bonus and a certain burden. Premature success gives one an almost mystical conception of destiny as opposed to will power—at its worst the Napoleonic delusion. The man who arrives young believes that he exercises his will because his star is shining. . . .
>
> The compensation of a very early success is a conviction that life is a romantic matter. In the best sense one stays young. When the primary objects of love and money could be taken for granted and a shaky eminence had lost its fascination, I had fair years to waste, years that I can't honestly regret, in seeking the eternal Carnival by the Sea.[2]

The Carnival by the Sea came later. For the present, there was enough of a carnival in the New York life Mr. and Mrs. Fitzgerald lived between April, 1920, and May, 1921. As Zelda described it in *Save Me the Waltz*—in an intended or unwitting parody of the beginning of "The Open Boat"—"Nobody knew whose party it was." The Fitzgeralds' life in New York was the kind one might expect of a newly married, newly rich couple who grew up founding their dreams "on the infinite promise of American advertising," and who both believed that "one can learn to play the piano by mail and that mud will give you a perfect complexion."[3]

I *Early Stories*

The early professional stories of Fitzgerald, those written shortly before and after *This Side of Paradise* was published, are collected in *Flappers and Philosophers* and *Tales of the Jazz Age*. Neither collection is as good as *Taps at Reveille*—Fitzgerald's last collection of short stories—and *Tales of the Jazz Age* suffers badly from the inclusion of some early writing which might better have remained in the *Nassau Lit*, where it first appeared. Together, *Flappers and Philosophers*, published September 10, 1920, five months after *This Side of Paradise*, and *Tales of the*

Jazz Age, published March 26, 1922, contain all but two of the stories Fitzgerald published in magazines in 1920 and 1921.

These two uncollected stories are "Myra Meets His Family," which appeared in the *Post* (March 20, 1920), and "The Smilers," in the *Smart Set* (June, 1920). "Myra" was written and rejected during those first frustrating months in New York. Though accepted after being revised, its omission from *Flappers and Philosophers* is for obvious reasons: "The Offshore Pirate," which was included, uses the same device. The device was to be used a third time and most successfully in "Rags Martin-Jones and the Pr-nce of W-les"; varied slightly, it did service in a fourth story, "Flight and Pursuit" (1932).

The device obviously appealed to Fitzgerald's theatrical nature: in an otherwise realistic story, the hero stages an elaborate fantasy complete in all its details and convincing to both the reader and the heroine of the story. In "Myra Meets His Family," the Fitzgerald woman, bored with men to the point of seeking a mate, fixes upon a young, wealthy, desirable chap, Knowleton Whiting, who is somewhat suspicious of her motives but blinded by her charms. The fantasy is the "family" Knowleton creates to test Myra's motives. It includes a run-down suburban estate, two hired actors, two dozen dogs, and a portrait of a Chinese ancestor. The trickster tricked, with which the story concludes, is Myra's way of revenge. Having discovered the plot and having secured Knowleton's apologies, she offers to marry him anyway. The marriage she arranges is as phony as Knowleton's "family," and she slips off the honeymoon train leaving him to discover his mistake somewhere past Buffalo. The closing line— "Tell the driver the Biltmore, Walter"—typifies the "flapper" story by which Fitzgerald won his dubious but imperishable reputation as "Chronicler of the Jazz Age."

The second was also a previously rejected story called "The Smilers" when it was published in *Smart Set*. The story is what Fitzgerald called a "plant" and is mercifully both short and buried deep in the magazine. The idea, however, relates to the serious concern Fitzgerald felt for truth as against appearances. The narrator begins by declaring himself against the smile which falsifies true feelings, and then the story shows through the main character how the world's sorrows lie in wait for the smilers and the misanthropes alike. In 1922, Fitzgerald expressed somewhat similar distaste for "the smilers" as part of an article "What I Think and Feel at Twenty-Five" in the *American Magazine.*

Still later, in 1925, he wrote a popular story about a mild-mannered cashier who tires of affecting politeness in the face of the world's rudeness and becomes momentarily famous as a "pusher-in-the-face," the title of the story. The idea, however, does not save either story from being a mere working out of a contrivance. It should be observed that "May Day," in the very next issue of *Smart Set,* showed Fitzgerald at his best.

Among the stories collected in *Flappers and Philosophers,* "The Ice Palace" is clearly the best and, in its way, as good a story as Fitzgerald ever wrote. It was the last to be written in the burst of energy which followed the acceptance of *This Side of Paradise.* Of the nine stories produced during that period, "Dalyrimple Goes Wrong," "Benediction," "The Cut-Glass Bowl," "Head and Shoulders," and "The Ice Palace" appeared in *Flappers and Philosophers.* "The Ice Palace," as Fitzgerald observed in "Early Success," was written with the professional's knack of making use of experience almost as it was going on. In an interview during these early years, Fitzgerald said the story grew out of two experiences. The one was a conversation with a St. Paul girl. " 'Here comes winter,' she said, as a scattering of confetti-like snow blew along the street. I thought immediately of the winters I had known there, their bleakness and dreariness and seemingly endless length. . . ." The other was with Zelda Sayre when he went to visit her in Montgomery shortly after his novel had been accepted. "She told me I would never understand how she felt about the Confederate graves, and I told her I understood so well that I could put it on paper. Next day on my way back to St. Paul it came to me that it was all one story. . . ."[4] The success of the story is in those observations: like all the best of Fitzgerald's work, "The Ice Palace" is created out of an intensely felt past, not only from recent moments of great emotional impact but from long-held feelings that go back into his youth.

The foremost characteristic of Fitzgerald's developing craft in this story is his use of the two contrasting settings to unify and intensify the story. Scene, milieu, and characters are blended so successfully that the reader finds himself not only engaged in the story but in the larger clash between two cultures, temperaments, and histories. By comparison with the use of setting and its relation to character and action in the Eleanor episode of *This Side of Paradise,* "The Ice Palace" is a great advance.

For all the contrast between North and South, Fitzgerald

does not lose touch with the reality of the individual cities—
St. Paul and Tarleton, Georgia—he is describing. In Sally Carrol
Happer, he creates one of his most convincing young girls,
individualizing her through a muted Southern accent which
seems always to find the words precisely appropriate to her
character. A tightly plotted story, it uses the right incidents to
illuminate character and has an inevitability that even a somewhat forced climax does not mar. Finally, the story is a long
one that hangs tightly together. The languorous scenes in Georgia
make it end where it began: the opening sentence, "The sunlight dripped over the house like golden paint over an art
jar," is exactly paralleled by the first sentence of the closing
section, "The wealth of golden sunlight poured a quite enervating
yet oddly comforting heat over the house. . . ." The story ends
with Sally Carrol and the best bit of dialogue in the story:

"What you doin?"
"Eatin' green peach. 'Spect to die any minute."

Perhaps the reason "The Ice Palace" is so successful is that
Fitzgerald not only infused the story with the tensions that
separated him from Zelda Sayre yet held him to her but also
with the warring strains in his own background: the potato-
famine Irish and the Maryland gentleman ancestry; the provincial and the Princetonian; poverty, cold, and control against
richness, ripeness, and passion.
    Of the other stories in *Flappers and Philosophers*, only "The
Cut-Glass Bowl" attempts a literary device somewhat similar to
the large contrasts in cultures in "The Ice Palace." Like "Benediction," it is a serious story, but longer and more ambitious.
The setting is St. Paul; the principal characters are Evelyn
Piper and her husband, Harold. The story takes place over
twenty-five years during which time Harold's business declines
and the Pipers' marriage degenerates into a "colorless antagonism." Its climactic events are melodramatic, and all are related
to the cut-glass bowl. Evelyn was given the bowl as a wedding
present from a disappointed suitor because she, too, was "hard,
beautiful, empty, and easy to see through." Evelyn's first (and
only) affair is discovered when the other man reveals his
presence by accidentally bumping into the bowl. Harold's
drunkenness is similarly dramatized. The daughter, Julie, cuts
her hand on the bowl and has to have it amputated. The letter
telling of the son's death in the war gets misplaced in the bowl.

Finally, Evelyn carries the bowl from the house, smashes it to earth, and falls upon it. In outline, such a story's faults appear clearly enough, and the Fitzgerald style and perception are not quite able to outweigh these defects. In addition, the story suffers from a habit which Fitzgerald had to discipline himself to overcome: the tendency to put himself into the characters and to urge their feelings rather than to disclose them through carefully chosen and precisely described actions.

"Benediction," as serious in its intent as it is slight in its effect, is a greatly changed version of "The Ordeal," which was published in the *Nassau Lit* (1915). The original story tried hard to dramatize convincingly the spiritual struggles of a boy of twenty about to take religious vows. At the moment of taking his vows, the boy is confronted with an immaterial yet powerful evil that has a way of turning up in other Fitzgerald stories. "Some evil presence," Fitzgerald wrote, "was in the chapel, on the very altar of God. . . . The eternity and infinity of all good seemed crushed, washed away in an eternity and infinity of evil."

Though the supernatural recurs fitfully in Fitzgerald's later work, very few of the stories and none of the novels after *This Side of Paradise* make explicit use of his Catholicism. The debate within him seems to have been written out (if not permanently stilled) in Amory's questionings in the novel. "The gaudy, ritualistic, paradoxical Catholicism whose prophet was Chesterton, whose claquers were such reformed rakes of literature as Huysmans and Bourget, whose American sponsor was Ralph Adams Cram, with his adulation of thirteenth-century cathedrals —a Catholicism which Amory found convenient and ready-made, without priest or sacrament or sacrifice" was unable to arouse even strong denial once this phase was over. Mention of it seldom appears in his notes or in any consequential way in his writings. At his death, his books were proscribed by the Church, and he was not permitted burial in hallowed ground. How little he knew of or felt for the religious life may explain the essential weakness of "Benediction." However, the moral concern and the sense of evil to be found in all his serious work may be important consequences of his youthful religious interest.

The other stories in *Flappers and Philosophers* are entertaining ones in which Fitzgerald indulges in his fondness for involved plots and ironic twists and relies upon characters close to himself and his experiences. "Bernice Bobs Her Hair" was the

first story, he observed in "Early Success," to provoke a large
number of letters. "For a shy man," he added, "it was nice to
be somebody except oneself again: to be 'the Author' as one had
been 'the Lieutenant.' Of course one wasn't really an author
any more than one had been an army officer, but nobody seemed
to guess behind the false face." One of Fitzgerald's great
strengths in his early work is the projection of this feeling into
his fiction: the world in which his characters live is both real and
fantastic, a bright, exciting world with no aggrieved past and
no wearying future. Such an attitude does not create "serious"
fiction, and Fitzgerald's "serious" stories here and to a certain extent later are less successful than his "light" ones. When,
as in "The Ice Palace," he could retain the manner of his
light stories and still invest the characters and events with
seriousness, he was moving in the direction of his best work.
As he developed his craft, the abandon with which Fitzgerald
created the rich imaginative details of the light story became
the detachment which made it possible for him to become
serious without becoming either sententious or wooden.

The contrast between "Bernice Bobs Her Hair," and "The Four
Fists" may add to what has just been said. In 1920, a story
could hardly have been better designed to elicit public response
than the Bernice story. Its characters are the college set; its
setting the comfortable middle class; its plot that of the ugly
duckling. The effect of the story depends upon how much the
reader is willing to let himself become engaged in the trans-
formation of Beatrice from the unattractive cousin to the girl
who bobs her hair. Its success is in the accuracy with which
Fitzgerald captured the world of the moment and made it seem
not necessarily important but terribly attractive. That attractiveness is only in part traceable to the story; in large part it is in
the writing, in the way things are said, the way they are
described. The story is not a great one; even by comparison
with similar stories, it is rather obviously contrived. But, in
not pretending to greatness, it pleases in that we get more than
we had a right to expect.

"The Four Fists" is quite the opposite. It, too, is a story
created out of a conventional, carefully contrived design, but
the over-all intent is serious. It creates a young male protagonist,
not unlike Basil in "The Freshest Boy," and shows the effects of
four physical blows upon his character. One blow was for snob-
bishness; the second, for personal unpleasantness; another, for

selfishness; and the last, for immorality. Character and situation are about as well created as they are in "Bernice Bobs Her Hair," but the reader, expecting more, gets much less. The story differs from the former one chiefly in that Fitzgerald was caught up in Bernice's world and in her emotions in a way he was not in those of Samuel Meredith in "The Four Fists." The reader feels the essential truth of the one—trivial as that truth may be—and the essential falsity of the other—profound as the sought truth may have been. It is testimony to Fitzgerald's awareness as a writer that "The Four Fists" irritated him almost as soon as he finished it and even after it had been widely praised. He wrote Maxwell Perkins: "Not that it is any cheaper than 'The Off-Shore Pirate' because it isn't, but simply because it's a plant, a moral tale and utterly lacks vitality."[5]

II *Fitzgerald and the Popular Magazine*

A close comparison between Fitzgerald's early light popular stories and his early serious ones reveals more weakness in the serious ones than in the others. Though Edmund Wilson could ask him for a realistic war story in 1919 with the appeal, "No *Saturday Evening Post* stuff, understand," and Fitzgerald himself could complain of the ease of selling a cheap story like "The Popular Girl" and the difficulty of selling "The Diamond as Big as the Ritz," the *Post* did not do badly by his early work. Nor is Arthur Mizener quite precise when he says his best work was hard to sell and implies that his mediocre work wasn't.

A glance at the magazines in which his early short fiction appeared suggests that good and bad appeared in both popular and quality magazines. Though *Smart Set* published "The Diamond as Big as the Ritz" after the story was refused by the *Post*, it also published "Mister Icky," "Tarquin at Cheapside," "Porcelain and Pink," and "Benediction," all as weak as any of the stories of these years. The *Post*, on the other hand, published "The Popular Girl," "Myra Meets His Family," "The Off-Shore Pirate," and a number of others somewhere between the bad and the competent, but it also published "The Ice Palace." *Scribner's*, more reputable than either of the other magazines— and more solemn—published "The Cut-Glass Bowl" and "The Four Fists," serious but weak fiction. Though the *Post* may be justly accused of encouraging Fitzgerald to turn out run-of-the-mill popular fiction for high prices (he wrote sixty-four *Post* stories), it did not indulge him in another direction he found easy to take: that of combining the melodramatic and the moral in ambitiously "serious" fiction.[6] Fitzgerald could protest against letting the *Post* have "Your Way and Mine" in 1926—"one of the lousiest stories I've ever written"—because he expected his *Post* stories to be of respectable quality. Two years later, it was the *Post* that took all of the Basil Duke Lee stories.

In the latest Scribner's collection of stories, which represents an attempt to cull out the best for college literature courses, three of the ten stories first appeared in the *Post,* two in *Smart Set,* two in the *American Mercury,* one in the *Metropolitan Magazine* (which also printed "The Jelly Bean" and *The Beautiful and Damned*), and one each in *Redbook* and *Esquire.* The general point that can be made about Fitzgerald and magazine fiction is that throughout the 1920's the popular magazines provided a large market for fiction and one whose requirements were not so far from those of the literary magazines of the day as that between the "slicks" and the "quality" magazines today. The *Post* published a good deal of bad fiction, much of it Fitzgerald's; but it also published some good writing by very good writers. In a weekly magazine running 190 pages and printing regularly eight or nine long stories and two serials by such writers as Fitzgerald, Ring Lardner, Sinclair Lewis, and Dorothy Parker, some good writing was bound to appear.

If there is a complaint to be made about Fitzgerald's tie to the popular magazine, it is probably that the *Post* and its counterparts did not encourage new directions in fiction. As time passes, at least with respect to Fitzgerald's short fiction, this begins to appear as much a virtue as a defect. To modern students, Fitzgerald's stories are old-fashioned in form[7] and leisurely in pace. Almost all are plot stories carefully directed toward a climax, fully created in both character and setting, and with the action often developing over a long span of time. They are, by comparison with modern popular fiction, long stories. Many of the stories that appeared in the *Post* ran to ten thousand words. A slight, early story like "Myra Meets His Family" went to almost thirteen thousand.

These attributes are not necessarily those of inferior fiction. The judicious question is how well the stories are done. For a novelist, as Fitzgerald liked to think of himself, the demand for long popular fiction called for more of the fullness and expansiveness associated with the novel. The defects of Fitzgerald as a short-story writer do not include sketchiness or dribble. His stories required careful structure (almost all are broken into three or more parts), and the space they unfold in offers more opportunities for the writer to practice his craft than the diffuse mood stories which were to become the standard pattern of the "new" fiction of Fitzgerald's time and after. Fitzgerald's natural skill, in this respect, can be measured by setting any one of his long, ambitious stories—"May Day," "Babylon Revisited, "The Rich Boy"—beside the long short stories which are the exception in Hemingway's work. The superiority, in this one respect at least, is clearly Fitzgerald's.

Fitzgerald's short fiction has suffered neglect because it seems so unaffected by the developments which were taking place in the short story. His weaknesses gain emphasis because they are related to the kind of short story which was out of favor even when it was well done. His reliance upon plot often forced the conclusion of a story or led it to a final twist that might have embarrassed O. Henry. The length of his stories sometimes leads to padding. The over-elaborate structure may be blamed upon a tendency to pursue—and not always clearly—several objectives within the same story. And, in sticking to the old-fashioned virtues, he may have relied too much on narration and situation rather than exploring the possibilities that indirection, understatement, symbolism, and conciseness were opening up to the short-story writer.

III *The Flapper and The Sheik*

An inescapable consequence of Fitzgerald's early stories was his identification with two type characters: the flapper and the sheik, the new woman and the Jazz Age young man. That identification complicated his being taken as a serious writer. In truth, the early stories offer few characters who do not fit the stereotype or disclose a variant of it: Sally Carrol Happer, Bernice, Rosalind, and Isabelle among the girls; Warren McIntyre, Amory, Bryan Dalyrimple among the men. Paradoxically, variants of these two "type" characters in his best fiction were so sharply individualized—and therefore memorable—that he became identified with the stereotype. In a way, he was the victim of his own great skill, somewhat in the reverse of the condition described in his notebooks:

When the first-rate author wants an exquisite heroine or a lovely morning, he finds that all the superlatives have been worn shoddy by his inferiors. It should be a rule that bad writers must start with plain heroines and ordinary mornings, and, if they are able, work up to something better.[8]

He created his best characters so well that all his inferior ones took on their characteristics. He was left, not with the handful of sharply individual characters he created, but with the generalized impression of having created one type.

"Even more puzzling to me—and I assume to all readers who were born too late to remember the Jazz Age," Mrs. Frances Fitzgerald Lanahan wrote in 1960, "is how my father came to be a symbol of it all (except much later, in retrospect, when his life seemed to parallel it so closely that he became woven into the legend of the era)." There are only two flappers in *Tales of the Jazz Age,* she claims, and one of these "belongs less to the flapper family than to the turn-of-the-century soubrettes of Paris."[9]

Perhaps the answer to the puzzlement of Mrs. Lanahan (now Scottie Fitzgerald Smith) lies in *This Side of Paradise* and in *Flappers and Philosophers.* Given Amory and Rosalind and Isabelle in the novel and the leading characters in half of the stories in *Flappers and Philosophers,* the reader can find enough common characteristics to identify Fitzgerald with them forever. More than that, the stories all appeared within a very short period of time, evidently a time when the public knew this kind of boy and that kind of girl and was receptive to seeing them described precisely and with such effortless skill. It is not in *Tales of the Jazz Age* that one finds the typical Jazz Age figures. They appear in the earlier stories, are almost limited to them, because Fitzgerald was committing his talent to that kind of story even as he was outgrowing it. The flapper, Fitzgerald himself said, had become passé by 1923. Two years later, *McCall's* had the Fitzgeralds tell the public "What Became of Our Flappers and Sheiks," with illustrations by John Held, Jr.

The quip about *This Side of Paradise,* "a book about flappers written for philosophers," which furnished the title for the short-story collection, is more accurate than most such glib phrases. Though the title came after the stories, it fits a good half of the stories in the collection and fits one exactly. This is "Head and Shoulders," the first story Fitzgerald sold to the movies; it has as its central characters a flapper and a philosopher; the girl, Marcia Meadows, is a very good example of Fitzgerald's flapper type.

Marcia is nineteen, "a blonde by natural pigment who wore no paint on the streets at high noon." She is the girl all the Yale students came to see do her song about the Jazz-Bound Blundering Blimp and a "shaky, shivery, celebrated dance." She is fond of pranks and not afraid to play outrageous ones. Her wit displays itself in remarks like, "I call you Omar because you remind me of a smoked cigarette." She smokes herself, yawns a good deal, and is fond of kissing, whether giving or receiving. She likes to be looked at and, while careless of her beauty, is so beautiful that she can afford to be. If her outward characteristics are designed to shock, her inner ones include a large measure of innocence and an instinctive though unconventional moral sense. She is no dumb blonde; Fitzgerald seldom creates such a character without endowing her with a good mind. In "Head and Shoulders" Marcia Meadows writes *Sandra Pepys, Syncopated,* a best-selling book through which she becomes "head" of the family. Marcia is, in short, a combination of those contrasting qualities Fitzgerald also admired in his male alter egos: naïveté and knowingness, strong reserve and unquenchable wit, indolence and energy, gaiety and sadness, brashness and humility. She is a long way from being the sentimental heroine of today's popular fiction: the prostitute with the heart of gold.

As the flapper appears in other early stories, she may vary slightly in one quality or another, may have one trait emphasized and another subdued, but her basic character remains consistent from one story to another. Bernice and Marjorie in "Bernice Bobs Her Hair" begin as opposites, then blend into one. At the end, Bernice proves superior to Marjorie, partly because Marjorie has done such an excellent job of tutoring her. Marjorie is described as "having a fairylike face and a dazzling bewildering tongue," and she is "justly celebrated for having turned five cart-wheels in succession during the last pump-and-slipper dance at New Haven." Bernice, being womanly, dainty in mind, and uncertain of her charms, is "out of style" in a way that challenges Marjorie to transform her. Having been forced, by Marjorie, into going through with bobbing her hair, Bernice retaliates by snipping off Marjorie's braids in her sleep and then tossing them on Warren McIntyre's porch. Thus, courage and daring are at the last added to Bernice's character to complete her development into a Fitzgerald girl.

Her name is Ardita in "The Off-Shore Pirate." She is again nineteen, "slender and supple, with a spoiled alluring mouth and quick gray eyes full of radiant curiosity." She reads Anatole France, says "darn," throws a book at her uncle; and yet, because of the "utter childishness of her beauty," she renders him "helpless, uncertain, utterly fatuous." When Toby Moreland decides to win her, he chooses to pose as a pirate and board the yacht on which Ardita has been idling her youth away. When he reveals his monstrous deception, she has to remain true to her own ideals and say, "What an imagination! I want you to lie to me just as sweetly as you know how for the rest of my life."

Sally Carrol Happer is different only in the attention the story gives to her Southern, small-city background. She smokes, says "damn," is fond of kissing, bobs her hair, makes witty remarks, engages in intellectual conversations, shocks her elders, and for all that, is, like the others, fundamentally, childishly innocent and eminently desirable.

The Fitzgerald male was similarly established in these early stories, but he did not become the central figure until the appearance of Amory Blaine in *This Side of Paradise*. In the stories just mentioned, only Toby Moreland in "The Off-Shore Pirate" is the equal of the girl being pursued, and in that story he appears for the most part in disguise. We can scarcely recall his name in "The Ice Palace." His general characteristics can be picked out in Warren McIntyre of "Beatrice Bobs Her Hair." "He was nineteen and rather pitying with those of his friends who had not gone East to college"; he was casually attending Yale. He worships Marjorie, though he fears she is faithless. He has a line, but he hates to be called "fresh" except in a joking way. He can be charitable as well as unkind, bored as well as impassioned. He is faintly superior to almost everyone, correct, handsome, too aware of bad form to be a parlor-snake but not sufficiently proper to be unattractive to the kind of girls we've been describing.

When the male of Fitzgerald's fiction becomes a fully developed character, he takes on certain eccentricities or peculiarities, distinctive traits of personality or family background, which bring him closer to the details of the author's past and make him a more interesting figure. Drunk, and he often is, he appears as Percy Parkhurst in "The Camel's Back," or Clark Darrow in

"The Jelly Bean," or Gordon Sterrett in "May Day," if we con-
fine the observation to stories written in 1920. Sober, he begins
to divide into two types: the rich boy who was born into his
eminence; and the boy, like Dexter Green in "Winter Dreams,"
who comes up the hard way. The latter affords a more interesting and fully understood character. Dexter, Nick Carraway, the
Jelly Bean, even Gatsby, belong to this type. Bryan Dalyrimple
in "Dalyrimple Goes Wrong" is the best example—and the best
male character—in the stories in *Flappers and Philosophers*.

Considered in relation to the Basil Lee stories, which were
not written until eight years later, Bryan is one possibility
into which Basil might have grown. To Basil, the idea of being
a gentleman burglar was always attractive; Bryan Dalyrimple
tries it out. (When he commits his first robbery, he, like Basil
confronting Hubert Blair, feels "morally alone.") Aside from its
rags-to-riches pattern, the story catches attention for the way
in which Fitzgerald conveys the feelings of the poor boy of intelligence and desire who is trying to make a break upward.
Bryan's father has lost his business; Bryan's education has ended
after two years at the state university. Despite his being a war
hero, he can find no job except that of stock boy in a wholesale
grocery. The most important characteristic of the Fitzgerald
male is to be found in Bryan's imaginative daring and in the
intensity and direction of his desires: "I'll go East—to a big city—
meet people—bigger people . . . My God, there *must* be a way."

Anson Hunter in "The Rich Boy" (not written until 1925) is
the best example of Fitzgerald's attempt to understand the man
for whom wealth is a natural right. In a way, the rich boy is
like a Platonic form; he lacks the substance to be found in the
struggling human being trying to shape itself into that ideal.
Much of Fitzgerald's examination of these dual characters was
concerned with trying to see clearly the values in both the ideal
and the copy. Intelligence, imagination, daring, courage, wit,
beauty, and strength are the youthful qualities he prized; almost
from the beginning of his fiction he prized wealth because that
seemed so obviously the condition under which these personal
qualities could flourish. What gives greater depth to his male
characters is what Nick Carraway describes at the beginning of
The Great Gatsby as "a sense of the fundamental decencies." On
the one hand, that sense is the basis for the morality none of
Fitzgerald's male characters can escape; on the other, it is the
invitation to the sin of pride to which all are drawn.

IV *"The Most Famous Young Writer in America"*

With as autobiographical a writer as Fitzgerald, the reality of his fictional characters, male or female, comes out of his incisive glances into himself. Their sameness explains itself there; the variations are explained in Fitzgerald's remark: "There never was a good biography of a good novelist. There couldn't be. He's too many people if he's any good." What comes through most of all in these early stories written in that brief glorious time of "early success" are the attractive men and the dazzling women, gloriously young and temporarily free.

"Scott Fitzgerald is the most famous young writer in America today," an article in the *American Magazine* announced in 1922. "Read his article if you want to understand Youth's point of view." The article, "What I Think and Feel at Twenty-Five," displayed a full-page portrait of the author, and in an inset on the first page, an excerpt from the article called "The Chief Thing I Have Learned So Far":

> If you believe in anything very strongly—including yourself— and if you go after that thing alone, you end up in jail, in heaven, in the headlines, or in the largest house in the block, according to what you started after. If you don't believe in anything very strongly—including yourself—you get along, and enough money is made out of you to buy an automobile for some other fellow's son, and you marry if you've got time, and if you do, you have a lot of children whether you have time or not, and finally you get tired and you die.[10]

As gloriously sudden as Fitzgerald's early success seems, it undoubtedly was in part a triumph of will, a persistence maintained against the common American notion that writing as a career was peculiar, profitless, and presumptive. When he reached sixty, Fitzgerald threatened in his article to "concoct a Scott Fitzgerald who will make a Benjamin Franklin look like a lucky devil who loafed into prominence." His present fame, he pointed out, had been won over the repeated warnings from family and friends against wanting to write at all, against thinking he could, and against publishing stories "about silly little boys and girls that nobody wants to read about." The image of himself as "Youth Triumphant" was a partial answer to his opposition. "The main thing," he wrote, "is to be your own kind of darn fool."

CHAPTER 4

A Touch of Disaster

AS THE MONEY flowed rapidly in and even more rapidly out, the life of the Fitzgeralds appears chiefly in the mixed truth and legends of splashings in the Plaza fountain, of riding down Fifth Avenue on the top of a taxi, of a second-hand Marmon driving into or out of New York headed for a party. An intoxicated life in both the literal and figurative sense, it was indulged in as if Fitzgerald were trying to sustain the ecstatic feeling that came with his first success. But despite the parties and sometimes even as they were going on, the professional writer worked.

The immediate question after *This Side of Paradise* was what to do next. In a letter written immediately after its acceptance, Fitzgerald proposed "a very ambitious novel . . . which will probably take a year" tentatively called *The Demon Lover*. The novel was not written, though the title appears in *The Beautiful and Damned* as the novel that brought Richard Caramel sudden fame. In October, he wrote to the editor of *Scribner's Magazine*, to whom he had just sold two stories, proposing a novelette out of his old journals to be called "The Diary of a Literary Failure." This, too, failed to materialize, and by the end of 1919 he was writing of a "frightful literary slump"—"a pumped-dry period," he called it later. He entertained the thought of doing a movie before another novel. In January, 1920, when he went to New Orleans, he had in mind still another novel to be called "Darling Heart." A part of that novel, Arthur Mizener speculates, may have been the affair between Anthony Patch and Dorothy Raycroft in *The Beautiful and Damned*. Not until late summer of 1920 did Fitzgerald have clearly in mind the novel, *The Flight of the Rocket*, which concerned the life of Anthony Patch who is wrecked "on the shoals of dissipation" between twenty-five and thirty-one. For the most part, his energies of this year were devoted to the short story, filling the demand created by having a half-dozen Jazz Age stories published in rapid succession during the first six months of 1920.

The self-portrait he wrote for the *Post* (September 18, 1920) is inaccurate in details but honest in the essential truth to the young writer, somewhat bewildered by success, but not too bewildered to take advantage of it. The sketch, in keeping with the personal touch demanded by the "Who's Who" series, is breezy, brash, yet appealing. Fitzgerald's early writing is magnified, his academic difficulties at the time of leaving Princeton forgotten, his failing grades reduced to mathematics and hygiene, and the writing of *This Side of Paradise* compressed into the consecutive weekends of three months. "Now," the sketch closes, "I spend my time wondering how it all happened."

The life of the Fitzgeralds between the appearance of *This Side of Paradise* in the spring of 1920 and *The Beautiful and Damned,* two years later, was almost as self-destructive as that of Anthony Patch and Gloria in the novel. It was reckless and careless, taxed by drinking and parties, redeemed by repeated attempts to find solid footing. As early as December, 1920, Fitzgerald found himself badly in debt; though he had earned $18,000 in the past year, he owed $1,600 and had little to show for his spending. Though he could make a good joke (and immediate cash) of it in "How to Live on $36,000 a Year,"[1] debts harassed him, drove him to work, aggravated the feeling of conflict between Zelda's (and his) immediate desires and his dream of being a great writer. Almost always, at least until the mid-1930's, money would arrive in time. There are many stories showing Fitzgerald's attitude toward money—leaving the Knickerbocker Hotel in 1919 with twenty- and fifty-dollar bills sticking from his vest and coat pockets, for example—and there is much evidence in his "Ledger," his letters, and his stories that the getting and spending of money was a serious matter, but one kept less so by a deliberate effort to treat it lightly.

The move to Westport, Connecticut, in May, 1920, was the first of many moves in search of an orderly life. For a time, life in the suburbs made the disappearance of money seem more mysterious but no less rapid. Nor did it cut down on the parties; it only stretched them out to and from New York and the house in Westport. Despite the life, Fitzgerald produced *The Beautiful and Damned* during 1920 and 1921, in time for it to begin serialization in the *Metropolitan Magazine* (September, 1921). In the period between the publication of *This Side of Paradise* and the book publication of *The Beautiful and Damned* (March 3, 1922), he wrote "May Day," a 23,000-word story and one of his best; "The Jelly-Bean," another excellent story; "The Curious Case of Benjamin Button"; "The Diamond as Big as the Ritz"; "O Russet Witch!"; and "The Lees of Happiness"—all ambitious, long stories varying in their success. It was no wonder that he compared a later period of meager production with this one: "If I'd written *The Beautiful and Damned* at the rate of 1000 words a day it would have taken me four years."

As it was, the novel was finished in less than a year, in time for the Fitzgeralds to take a trip abroad in May, 1921. The departure of Anthony Patch for Europe at the close of the book is a kind of exaggerated portrait of Fitzgerald himself sinking into a deck chair exhausted from the steady drain of success. The trip was short and apparently not very satisfactory. Neither France nor England nor Italy impressed them, and they were back in the United States before three months had elapsed. Of most literary interest during this trip were Fitzgerald's meeting with Galsworthy and his attempt to see Anatole France. He paid Galsworthy the extravagant compliment of placing him with Joseph Conrad and Anatole France as the three living writers he most admired.

Upon their return to Montgomery, Alabama, in late July, 1921, they wavered between settling there or in St. Paul. Returning to New York was apparently out of the question for the time. "We played safe and went home to St. Paul," Fitzgerald wrote later. "It seemed inappropriate to bring a baby into all that glamor and loneliness. But in a year we were back and we began doing the same things over again and not liking them so much."[2] During the fourteen months they lived in St. Paul, Frances Scott Fitzgerald was born (October 26, 1921); *The Beautiful and Damned* was published in book form in March (they spent most of the month in New York); and the third collection of short stories, *Tales of the Jazz Age,* appeared September 10, 1922. In October, they moved back to New York, this time to the rented house in Great Neck, Long Island, which was to provide, in a general way, the setting for *The Great Gatsby.*

I *The Beautiful and Damned*

Looking back on these years, the "greatest, gaudiest spree in history," Fitzgerald wrote in 1937: "All the stories that came into my head had a touch of disaster in them—the lovely young creatures in my novels went to ruin, the diamond mountains

of my short stories blew up, my millionaires were as beautiful
and damned as Thomas Hardy's peasants."[3] If he had been
able to get that feeling convincingly into *The Beautiful and
Damned*, it would be a better novel than it is. But the touch
of disaster Fitzgerald was able to convey in it in 1922 seems
more literary than real; when it touches reality, it proves to be
more pathetic than tragic. His feeling for disaster is akin to
that of a Mrs. Smith in his notebooks; she "had been born on the
edge of an imaginary precipice and had lived there ever since,
looking over the precipice every half hour in horror, and yet
unable to get herself away."[4]

In a technical way, *The Beautiful and Damned* is a better
novel than *This Side of Paradise*. The book is orderly, the
material divided into three books and nine chapters. Fitzgerald
sticks to prose narrative and dialogue for the most part, and he
maintains a consistent tone and point of view. The story is
moderately interesting, and intermixed with the story of Anthony's
decline is a serious attempt to explore the character of a man
spoiled by the presence or promise of wealth. In addition, the
novel shows perceptive concern for the divided nature of the
attraction between a man and woman. The book's main weakness—and it is a devastating one—is that the central characters
Anthony Patch and Gloria Gilbert only feebly enlist the reader's
interest or sympathy.

Anthony Patch is a first version of Anson Hunter, the rich
boy in the story of that name whom Fitzgerald was to create
much more successfully four years later. Anthony has always
had enough money to put down any pressing necessity to work,
but apparently not enough to keep him from feeling some need
for a vocation. His marriage to Gloria forces him to live beyond
his means or to conform to a middle-class standard and way
of living. The promise of a multi-million dollar inheritance when
Adam Patch, his grandfather, dies is a device borrowed from the
Victorian novel; but Fitzgerald makes of it a kind of lure somehow associated with the ideal beauty which draws Anthony to
Gloria. The plot, at any rate, comes close to turning into
Victorian melodrama with an ironic and moralistic ending.
When Adam Patch happens upon a characteristically drunken
party at the Patch's little gray home in Marietta, he cuts Anthony
out of his will. After Adam's death, Anthony contests the will.
At the end of the novel, he wins the appeal only to have his
mind snap at the moment the favorable decision is announced.

The book ends with Anthony being brought on board *The Berengaria* in a wheel chair; he is still trying to justify his actions which had caused the rival claimant to Adam Patch's fortune to shoot himself. " 'I showed them,' he was saying, 'It was a hard fight, but I didn't give up and I came through!' "

Though there is more imagination and less reliance upon biography than in *This Side of Paradise,* the novel draws heavily upon the Fitzgeralds' experiences, particularly in the middle and final sections of the book. As a result, the central narrative is often interrupted, as it was in *This Side of Paradise,* by stories the author felt were too good to leave out. The story of the house guest and the Japanese butler is one; it derived from George Jean Nathan's whimsy that the Fitzgerald's Japanese houseboy was a German spy and from a series of variations he worked on that theme. Most of these interpolations are like this one: they not only add little to the novel but create the suspicion that such incidents are included merely to pad the book and to lengthen the distance between Anthony's wan beginning and woeful end.

Fitzgerald was only partially justified in resenting the fact that Anthony and Gloria on the jacket illustration looked so much like himself and Zelda. If the specifications—height, color of hair, facial structure—fit Fitzgerald more than the Anthony Patch described in the novel, it may be because Anthony seems to be more Fitzgerald than the self-consciously created fictional person he was supposed to be in the novel. Particularly is this true of Anthony after his marriage, and the shifting of Fitzgerald's experiences as a best-selling young novelist to Dick Caramel in the novel does not disguise the fact. Autobiographical material is extensive in *The Beautiful and Damned;* one of the faults of the book is Fitzgerald's inability to keep Anthony Patch and Gloria at a distance after the first third of the book.

For the readers of the time, the Fitzgeralds' lives were rather constantly before them. In 1922 to 1924, subscribers to the *American Magazine, Ladies' Home Journal, Vanity Fair, Motor, McCall's,* the *Post,* and *Woman's Home Companion* could read about the Fitzgeralds in articles ranging from "The Most Disgraceful Thing I Ever Did," to "Wait Till You Have Children of Your Own." In a magazine like the *Ladies' Home Journal,* which still featured fully illustrated articles about William Cullen Bryant by William Lyon Phelps, Fitzgerald's views were presented with some caution: "Mr. Fitzgerald is one of the most brilliant writers of the modernist school; and his article 'Imagination—and a Few Mothers' is published solely as a representation of the modernist viewpoint." The article was harmless enough, as were the others in the popular magazines, though Fitzgerald's manner was deliberately iconoclastic in most of the pieces he wrote. The domination of children by their parents or by women in the culture was a favorite subject. The ladies of the Lucy Stone League, he reported in one of his articles, were greatly shocked when he told them "most American boys learned to lie at some lady teacher's knee."[5] In all of these articles, the Fitzgeralds appeared in various poses. When he published his first story in *Hearst's International* in May, 1923, the magazine featured a full-page portrait with accompanying text, "Mrs. F. Scott Fitzgerald started the flapper movement in this country. So says her husband, the best-loved author of the younger generation."

These articles, stories in the newspapers, and at least the middle section of *The Beautiful and Damned* strengthened the stereotype of "flappers and philosophers" already created in Fitzgerald's earlier stories. Gloria, in marriage and out, has the outward characteristics that went with the flapper: a disdain for convention; a long list of admirers; a facile wit; a hard, brilliant, unwomanly beauty. Similarly, *The Beautiful and Damned* has a strong overdose of philosophy, from the brief and usually unsatisfactory attempts by Anthony to understand himself to the unbearable early-morning disquisition by Maury Noble. That Fitzgerald took these passages seriously is evidenced by a letter to Edmund Wilson, who had pointed out that in the "midnight symposium" none of the characters had anything to say. The revised material that Fitzgerald wrote to meet Wilson's objection is pretty much Maury Noble's speech as it now stands in the book. The early 1920's was, among other things, a talkative age.

Much more than *This Side of Paradise* and even more than his serious short stories that didn't come off, *The Beautiful and Damned* is a failure. "The story of Gloria and Anthony," Arthur Mizener concluded, "is full of precisely observed life, and Fitzgerald makes us feel the grief they suffer; but he is able to provide neither an adequate cause for their suffering nor adequate grounds in their characters for the importance he gives it."[6] The tragic vision is there, occasionally peering deep and conveying both the image and the feeling; but the gaze is fitful, too often distracted, and never quite certain how to regard the main characters it should focus upon.

Fitzgerald expected much of the novel, but the conditions under which it was written, the hurried feeling in it and in everything else he was writing at the time, the strain of recording experiences almost as they happened, may have forewarned him of its weaknesses. A letter to John Peale Bishop in the spring of the book's publication includes a long list of specific questions: Are the characters convincing? Is the style too ornate? Does the emotion come through? How about the humor—and the ideas? Is it boring or interesting? Is it imitative and of whom?

Part of this anxiety toward the novel reflects Fitzgerald's self-consciousness as an author, a self-consciousness heightened by his having deliberately created a serious novel in a very short time out of experiences which had had little time to work within him. By the time of the publication of the novel, Fitzgerald had been sufficiently advertised as a writer to make him even more self-conscious than he naturally was. *This Side of Paradise* had been reviewed with the kind of enthusiasm which often greets the first novel of promise; the second was likely to be looked to for confirmation of that favorable judgment. In January, 1922, Fitzgerald wrote to Edmund Wilson about a forthcoming sketch of him that Wilson was writing for *The Bookman*: "My curiosity is at fever heat—for God's sake send me a copy immediately."

The essay, as honest as Edmund Wilson always was about Fitzgerald's work, gave Fitzgerald the most perceptive and sharp criticism he had yet received. Wilson wrote:

> He has been given imagination without intellectual control of it; he has been given a desire for beauty without an aesthetic ideal; and he has been given a gift for expression without many ideas to express.
>
> In college, he had supposed the thing to do was to write biographical novels with a burst of ideas toward the close; since his advent into the literary world, he has discovered that there is another genre in favor: the kind which makes much of the tragedy and "the meaninglessness of life."[7]

Wilson's criticism was gentle in comparison with Burton Rascoe's in the same issue. He called the novel "blubberingly sentimental," and charged Fitzgerald with being "not only a novelist, but at the same time, an amateur philosopher, sociologist, and theologian.

. . . No one of late years has had more promising narrative talent and no one ever collapsed so easily into the banal and commonplace."

Harsh as it is, Rascoe's criticism is exactly to the point. Fitzgerald was not prepared to write serious fiction, he had no real idea of how to go about it, and he invariably disclosed his weaknesses when he became serious. Of all his short fiction to this time, "May Day" is the only story that manages to be both serious and convincing; and it is so chiefly because Fitzgerald kept the narrative and the characters steadily and persuasively before the reader. A story like "The Jelly-Bean" succeeds in conveying a seriousness beneath the lightness of the surface precisely because adopting the light manner kept Fitzgerald from losing the strength of character and action in a forced attempt to be "serious." If we contrast either story with "The Lees of Happiness," written at the same time, we see what the desire to write the "serious" story could do to Fitzgerald's natural gifts.

II   *Tales of the Jazz Age*

Tales of the Jazz Age is a more varied collection of short stories than *Flappers and Philosophers;* it is also a more interesting one because of its bearing upon Fitzgerald's development as a writer; but, perhaps because he needed stories to pad out the volume, it is a very uneven collection. "May Day," "The Diamond as Big as the Ritz," and "The Jelly-Bean" belong among his best stories. "Tarquin of Cheapside," "Mr. Icky," and "Jemina" are undergraduate sketches, and "The Lees of Happiness" is weak in its pretensions to seriousness.

In the original edition, the table of contents of *Tales of the Jazz Age* included Fitzgerald's offhand comments about each of the stories. "The Camel's Back," according to his note, was the story he liked least, though it was the easiest to write and gave him the most amusement. "The Diamond as Big as the Ritz" was the favorite story of a well-known critic, but Fitzgerald claimed to prefer "The Off-Shore Pirate." (In a letter written six months earlier he put this story among his cheap stories.) "O Russet Witch!" was written just after completing the first draft of *The Beautiful and Damned* when he was "somewhat carried away by the feeling that there was no ordered scheme to which he must conform." "The Lees of Happiness," he said, "will be accused perhaps of being a mere piece of sentimentality." The three short pieces were dismissed as ephemera. Except for the expressed liking for "The Off-Shore Pirate," his comments seem to be both candid and discerning.

"My Last Flappers" is the title given to the first four stories in the book: "The Jelly-Bean," "The Camel's Back," "Porcelain and Pink," and "May Day." "The Jelly-Bean" is an excellent story, a kind of Southern version of "Winter Dreams," cut off at the point where the provincial poor boy has met the ineffable rich girl and before he goes on to success. The boy is "the Jelly-Bean," Jim Powell; the girl is Nancy Lamar, who "had a mouth like a remembered kiss." Jim is a precisely sketched member of the lower middle class, an unambitious mechanic living over a garage when the story begins. Characteristically, however, his family was a good Southern one in days past, and at the end, he is planning to buy up a piece of land with the small inheritance he has received. Fitzgerald need not have provided his central character with such an ancestry, for the story concentrates on the feelings of an attractive, intelligent boy, in a tolerant small town, who discovers what being on the wrong side of the tracks means.

The story is in Fitzgerald's best casual manner. By this time, his stories frequently begin with a kind of address to the reader—a display piece whereby the author catches the reader's attention by revealing his personality in relation to some aspect of the story. The device could have been borrowed from a number of contemporary writers: Ring Lardner was using it more deftly than anyone else in the popular magazines of the time. In this story, the display piece is about the term "jelly-bean," "the name throughout the undissolved Confederacy for one who spends his life conjugating the verb *to idle* in the first person singular—I am idling, I have idled, I will idle."

Most of Fitzgerald's stories are oblivious to the world of menial, dull, deadly work which runs beneath the world his golden girls occupy. And yet, like the image of green Princeton set down amidst festering swamps and industrial blight, Fitzgerald's light, gay, middle- and upper-class world is from time to time juxtaposed with the world of vice, poverty, and boredom. "The Jelly-Bean" is set against the background of both worlds. Though the dark South does not explicitly appear in the story, it hovers at the edge; it is to be found in a story of the South Fitzgerald published in the *Metropolitan Magazine* during the same period: "That's my picture of the South now, you know—a skinny, dark-haired young man with a gun on his hip and a stomach full of corn liquor or Dope Dola, leaning up against a drug store waiting for the next lynching."[8]

When Fitzgerald turned to the character of the Jelly-Bean again in a story entitled "Dice, Brass Knuckles and Guitar," he made him a caricature in a contrived story whose few virtues reside in the fragments that Fitzgerald saved for inclusion in his notebooks:

> "Yes mam, if necessary. Look here, you take a girl and she goes into some cafe where she's got no business to go. Well, then, her escort he gets a little too much to drink an' he goes to sleep an' then some fella comes up and says, 'Hello, sweet mamma,' or whatever one of those mashers says up here. What does she do? She can't scream, on account of no real lady will scream nowadays—no—she just reaches down in her pocket and slips her fingers into a pair of Powell's defensive brass-knuckles, debutante's size, executes what I call the Society Hook, and Wham! that big fella's on his way to the cellar."[9]

In the two early novels, the world of toil and want is shallowly used to give Amory Blaine and Anthony Patch the occasion for wrinkling their nostrils and backing away. In both, the hatred of poverty, the ugliness of it, and the utter impossibility of it for superior beings come through in an honest but somewhat unpleasant way. There is not enough understanding to provoke sympathy, nor enough sympathy to lead to much understanding.

Gordon Sterrett's situation in "May Day" is more intense than that of Jim Powell in "The Jelly-Bean," but it is the same kind. Both, having been exposed to a world beyond their own, must try to come to terms with that vision. "May Day," ending as it does in Gordon Sterrett's suicide, is the starkest of Fitzgerald's early stories. In its episodic character and its seriousness it evinces the faults of the two novels, but the skill Fitzgerald displays in marshaling large scenes, in keeping background and continuing action nicely balanced, and in tying the disparate elements of the story closely together is admirable. Though his characters from the lower depths—Carrol Key and Gus Rose —are as much from literature as from life, they are used effectively. For all the contrived relationship between Edith Bradin, the Fitzgerald girl, and her brother Henry, the young idealist

who works on a Socialist newspaper, the atmosphere of the
May Day riots is powerfully created.

For a writer not used to depicting violence, the mob's attack on the *New York Trumpet,* Key's fall from the window,
Gordon's suicide, are all done with restraint without losing
impact. In the end, we might quarrel about the character of
Gordon Sterrett, the young provincial artist with the vision of
debutante beauty clouding his eyes and his mind. Readers of
Fitzgerald's earlier fiction are likely to find him fitting a standard
pattern, though his appearance in this story arouses more
response than one might expect. His suicide comes as a shock;
like Judge Brack in *Hedda Gabler,* the reader attuned to
Fitzgerald's conventional characters is likely to say, "People don't
do such things."

What passes muster in "May Day" does not get by in "The
Lees of Happiness." Fitzgerald said the story came to him in an
irresistible form, crying to be written. It is a short story, as
Fitzgerald's stories go, and yet it covers some dozen years in
the lives of four principal characters. As Fitzgerald seemed aware
in the introductory note, the story is pure melodrama. A young
writer, like Fitzgerald, marries a young girl, like Zelda Sayre.
At the peak of his early success, he develops a brain tumor which
dooms his wife, Roxanne, to caring for him during his vegetable
existence for eleven years. Running parallel to these events is
the unsuccessful marriage of a close friend, Harry, to a girl,
Kitty, who, for all her physical charms, turns out to be dirty,
lazy, and expensive. Kitty leaves Harry, and they are divorced
shortly after the principal character suffers the brain tumor.
After the writer's death, Harry and Roxanne both reflect upon
the cruelties life has inflicted, but neither is willing to try to
find happiness again with the other. Fitzgerald's usual per-
ceptiveness is in this story mere sententiousness, found in passages like, "To these two, life had come quickly and gone,
leaving not bitterness but pity, not disillusion, but only passion."
Where the story has any strength at all, it is in observations
about the young writer's work: "here were passably amusing
stories, a bit out of date now, but doubtless the sort that would
then have whiled away a dreary half hour in a dental office";
in such incidental details as Kitty's uncleanliness and Roxanne's
inept attempts to help her; and in such farcical touches as nailing
the bride's biscuits in a frieze around the kitchen. But even these
minor amusements do not save the story from being the kind

that deserves to remain in *The Chicago Tribune*, where it first appeared.

The fantasies in *Tales of the Jazz Age* are skillfully done, and "The Diamond as Big as the Ritz" is likely to remain as an outstanding story among modern stories of its kind. Of "O Russet Witch!," on the other hand, we never know whether it intends to be a fantasy or a realistic story, to be serious or merely diverting. Its theme is the transience of youth and the passing of youthful desires. Its moral fits a collection of stories about the Jazz Age. The central character, now a grandfather, "had angered Providence by resisting too many temptations. There was nothing left but heaven, where he would meet only those who, like him, had wasted earth." "Benjamin Button" plays upon the same idea; its plot was created from a remark of Mark Twain that it was a pity that the best part of life came at the beginning and the worst at the end. To accommodate this idea, Fitzgerald has Benjamin Button born to his Baltimore parents at the age (*Benjamin's* age) of seventy. His life marches from there to infancy, and the story is not so remarkable in its telling as in the fact that Fitzgerald stuck to it all the way through. It was the kind of story which provoked a response Fitzgerald printed in the table of contents: "Sir—I have read the story 'Benjamin Button' in *Collier's* and I wish to say that as a short story writer you would make a good lunatic. . . ."

"Tarquin of Cheapside" tells how Shakespeare wrote "The Rape of Lucrece." The setting is sixteenth-century London, and the central character, a friend of Shakespeare, hides him from a brother bent on avenging his sister's defilement. Stated thus bluntly, the story may have justified Maxwell Perkins' wish to keep it out of the collection because he thought the story morally offensive. The handling of the situation, however, makes Perkins seem unduly prissy in that respect and unduly tolerant in respect to its literary offensiveness.

"The Diamond as Big as the Ritz" has become one of Fitzgerald's most celebrated stories, partly because of its merit and partly because it is so useful for discussing Fitzgerald's attitude toward money and American materialism. Putting aside the second point for a moment, let us look at the story. The situation is brilliantly set forth. A sketchy background using a variety of obvious thematic names—the Ungers from Hades, St. Midas' school, Percy Washington—brings the story to the thesis statement, delivered by Percy, "That's nothing at all. My father has a diamond bigger than the Ritz-Carlton Hotel." There is, despite considerable Fitzgerald foolery, more serious satire in the story than in the other fantasies. The forbidding village of Fish with the twelve men who "sucked a lean milk from the almost literally bare rock," is one vision of the barren materialistic world Fitzgerald saw beneath the very surface of the American life that his stories most often described. The kingdom of Braddock Washington, with his rococo motion-picture chateau, his unmatchable wealth, and his slaves is the vision of Heaven that the undernourished American imagination most often envisions. The climax of the story is the attack upon Washington's kingdom and his attempt to bribe God—"God had his price, of course." But God refuses the bribe; the dream ends with the young man, John Unger, escaping from the mountains with Kismine and Jasmine, Braddock Washington's two daughters. The wealth of John Unger's dreams has escaped him, and he ends with second-best—the sentimental romance of the beautiful and empty-headed girl, "with one dress and a penniless fiancé." At the end, we arrive very close to the Fitzgerald of *The Great Gatsby*. Gatsby had to be "about his Father's business, the service of a vast, vulgar, and meretricious beauty." In the course of that novel, Fitzgerald explores thoroughly not only the cheapness and tawdriness of Gatsby's desires, but the essential greatness of Gatsby's vision, of any vision which proves superior to the objects it fastens upon.

In "The Diamond as Big as the Ritz," Fitzgerald's perception is neither so broad nor so unified as it was to become in the novel. What the story does most successfully is to assert some fundamental beliefs that Fitzgerald had already hinted at in other stories: that poverty is dull, degrading, and terrifying, and irremediable by pious homilies about the blessed poor; that money is no more the root of all evil than is the absence of it; that evil has a way of pushing in on everyone, rich or poor; that the rich probably have a better chance of getting something from life before it gets them than the poor; and that youth is the most precious form of wealth and even that is somewhat non-negotiable without the fact of or the illusion of wealth and beauty. There is a good deal of brimstone to be found in "The Diamond as Big as the Ritz," despite the hero's final assertion: "Your father is dead. Why should he go to Hades? You have it confused with another place that was abolished long ago."

The end of "The Diamond as Big as the Ritz" may seem to

back away from the harsher implications of the story into a conventional boy and girl ending. But such a conclusion tends to
gloss over the fact that, throughout the story, the romance and
the satire are tightly interwoven, the one providing the surface
which teases the imagination, the other suggesting the depths beneath. A recent critic has argued that the sentimentality of the
romantic ending is played off against that of the dream images
which precede it.[10] The emotional extravagance of the dream
is comparable to the emotional cheapness of the romance; "they
are both equally the products of the same sensibility."

III *The Vegetable*

Fitzgerald's fondness for satire which helped attract him to
Samuel Butler, Shaw, and H. G. Wells shows itself in all his
work. But the satirical spirit seemed to work fitfully and at
varying degrees of intensity. He was never sufficiently committed
to one scheme of things or another, never sufficiently bitter or
sufficiently animated toward reform, to put his energies into
sustained social satire. Satire was chiefly a device to be used
to pick up interest when the narrative slowed down, or to
show off a character's satirical wit, or to let the author's imagination roam free after laboring over a novel or a similarly sustained
piece of work. In his short fiction and his novels, he was too
much the observer of his inner and outer states and of the
events through which he passed to become the satirist spurred
by fierce, yet controlled, hates. He had to write from the
particulars to the general, from the individual character to the
type rather than from the general intention of satire to the
particulars of character and incident to bring it out.

The Vegetable, or From President to Postman, Fitzgerald's
next published work after *Tales of the Jazz Age,* suffers
from being born out of a satirical intent which the author is
never able to dramatize effectively. The motivations behind the
play—Fitzgerald's only mature attempt at drama—are many and
help to account for its mixed character. Drama was, in a way,
Fitzgerald's forte. Self-dramatization had become a habit with
him, at least as early as his going to Newman. His juvenile
writing invariably falls into dramatic form. And not until *The
Great Gatsby* could he convince himself that a play imbedded
in a novel was not necessarily diverting to the reader. He wrote
dialogue superbly and many of his characters seemed ready to

step on the stage. In 1962, a dramatization of *This Side of Paradise* was one of the most successful off-Broadway productions.

Like all fashionable New Yorkers, the Fitzgeralds attended the theater frequently; they knew theater people; and undoubtedly writing for the theater had more appeal to Fitzgerald than writing for the popular magazines. In addition, there was the alluring possibility that a hit play would make a great deal of money. When his interest in trying a play turned to the actual writing of one, the thought of making money was strongly in mind. He wrote to Perkins early in 1922 "of an awfully funny play that's going to make me rich forever."

He was at work on a play as early as 1921; and, when *The Beautiful and Damned* was completed, he turned to it again and evidently brought it into shape by the spring of 1922. He was calling it *Gabriel's Trombone* during the summer. Though he continued to work on it, he was also thinking about a new novel and loafing more than he ever did when a real idea was upon him. The play, rejected in the fall of 1922, was rewritten again during the first months back in New York after their long stay in St. Paul. The late months of 1922 and most of 1923 were not among Fitzgerald's most productive times. The total published work in 1923 was *The Vegetable*, two poor stories, and two mediocre articles.

The Vegetable in its final published form is not the kind of work that seems likely to have drawn from Fitzgerald more than a fraction of his talent and energy. We surmise that, despite the rewriting that went into it, *The Vegetable* is but an extension of much of the talk that flowed through the parties of the winter and spring of 1922-23. The play was finally accepted in October, and Fitzgerald became engrossed in the details of production. Ernest Truex opened in the leading role, and Fitzgerald and his friends went to Atlantic City to see it try out. Fitzgerald called it a "total frost" and spent the second and third acts in a bar. The show never reached Broadway.

Fitzgerald's judgment that the play was hopeless has never been challenged by later readers. The reasons for its badness are worth considering. It is probably not so much a failure of intent—"Of Thee I Sing" made similar political satire highly effective—as of execution.[11] The plot, and it has none of importance, shows a $3000-a-year clerk named Jerry Frost becoming President overnight. After a brief period as President he reverts back to his former existence, this time as a postman, a position which he had long desired and which brings him happiness. These events fit the three acts, Act One taking place in the living room of the Frosts' house, Act Two shifting to the White House, and Act Three returning to the Frosts' living room.

What the play chiefly lacks is body for the political satire. The characters were not intended to be more than vehicles for that satire; therefore they do not engage the audience's interest in character development or actions. Fitzgerald had expressed himself about American politics in *The Beautiful and Damned* almost as extensively as in *The Vegetable*: his opinion in the novel was that any nincompoop could be President; that politics was a grubby business; and that no intelligent man would go near it. *The Vegetable*, which says very little more, doesn't make its message either dramatic or interesting. The second-act fantasy with Jerry and his relatives in the White House is no better than the first act which sought its comic effects in bad puns and bad jokes (occasionally passed off *as* bad jokes) about popular taste and bootleggers.

It comes as something of a surpise to anyone who reads past the second act of *The Vegetable* to find that the play ends wistfully. For, paralleling the main satire is a good deal that reflects the Fitzgeralds' domestic life as surely as did *The Beautiful and Damned*. The two most prolonged jokes in the play are those about Jerry Frost and his bootlegger and Jerry Frost and the quarrel with his wife. The last act of the play is chiefly concerned with Jerry's disappearance after he leaves the White House. When Jerry returns as the postman, he is not recognized, and he engages his wife in a long conversation about her missing husband. In the course of her promises to be a better wife when he comes back, the postman gives her a letter from Jerry: "It just says he's well and comfortable. And that he's doing what he wants to do and what he's got to do. And he says that doing his work makes him happy." Fitzgerald's feelings were stronger when he described to his daughter in 1938 the effects of his own marriage: "I was divided," he wrote; "she wanted me to work for her and not enough for my dream."

Regarded as an entity, *The Vegetable* suffers from the intrusion of Fitzgerald's immediate life in the same way that *The Beautiful and Damned* suffers. A good portion of the middle part of the novel (when it most loses its sense of direction) is a transcription of Fitzgerald's difficulty in doing his work amidst a continuing party and with a wife who was something of a rival. Anthony is as pathetic in trying to establish himself as a man who has work to do and who must be left alone to do it as Jerry Frost is wistful. The conflict is a commonplace one, but neither Fitzgerald nor Zelda were commonplace people. Much of the time, their marriage must have divided itself into his work and her life. The blame is not all hers, of course; their undisciplined life was a joint creation.

Nevertheless, by the time he had written two novels and a number of good stories, he had developed a deeper sense of vocation that that of the days when he was writing *This Side of Paradise* to win the girl and the jackpot. Ironically, four years later Zelda was the one to develop the overpowering sense of dedication and to marshal the will to pursue it. But her obsession with dancing was pathological, and it came at a time when Fitzgerald's ability to dedicate himself to writing was never more seriously in doubt. The picture, in Zelda's *Save Me the Waltz* (1932), of David Knight assuming the management of the family while Alabama pursues her dancing career is a kind of bitter caricature faintly anticipated in the troubles both of Jerry Frost and of Anthony Patch.

The anecdotes which illuminate the Fitzgeralds' lives on Long Island in 1923-24 are not much different from those of 1920-21, but they are less funny and more desperate. As Fitzgerald put it, "We began doing the same things over again and not liking them so much. . . . By this time we knew everybody. . . . But we were no longer important." The Fitzgeralds who seem to be so closely identified with New York City in the 1920's are really a couple without a permanent address. The events in their lives go by so fast that the observation of Mrs. Frances Fitzgerald Lanahan that her father's contemporaries must have lived forty-eight hours for every twenty-four hours of clock time seems almost precisely correct. When these events are used in Fitzgerald's fiction, the actual time is usually stretched out to make the scene plausible. The first gaudy sprees in New York after their marriage, which Fitzgerald stretches out to three months in writing about them, lasted a mere matter of weeks. Again, the period in the suburbs described in *The Beautiful and Damned* lasts two years (with winter in an apartment in New York). The Fitzgeralds actually stayed in Westport only one summer, moved into the city for the winter, and left for Europe the following May. Despite the identification of the Fitzgeralds with New York, their residence in St. Paul in 1921 and 1922 was for almost as long a period as that spent in the New York suburbs in 1922 and 1923.

When the Anthony Patches leave for Europe, seven years have elapsed since their marriage. When the Fitzgeralds left the second time—May, 1924—only four years had gone by. But, though Fitzgerald must have been feeling almost as enervated as Anthony Patch, he was taking with him the hope of writing a novel far better than anything he had yet done.

CHAPTER 5

The Great Gatsby

MY BOOK is wonderful"—Fitzgerald wrote Edmund Wilson from France in the fall of 1924—"so is the air & the sea. I have got my health back—I no longer cough and itch and roll from one side of the bed to the other all night and have a hollow ache in my stomach after two cups of black coffee. I really worked hard as hell last winter—but it was all trash and it nearly broke my heart as well as my iron constitution."[1]

This book was *The Great Gatsby*. The hard work was the eleven stories and articles Fitzgerald wrote in six months to get himself out of debt after the failure of *The Vegetable*. When he finished these in April, he had just over seven thousand dollars, enough to get them to France and to keep them while he worked on the serious writing he desperately wanted to do.

The years in Great Neck had not been a total loss. They furnished setting and tone for *The Great Gatsby*, and they strengthened his resolve to be more than a fashionable magazine writer. Moreover, the most important personal acquaintance of these years had been a literary one, Ring Lardner, then thirty-eight and living nearby. Fitzgerald's tribute to him "Ring" (1933)[2] is the only extended piece he wrote about a literary man, and his interest in Lardner's work in 1923 was largely responsible for the publication of a collection of Lardner's stories, "How to Write Short Stories" (1924). Among other reasons for the closeness of the two writers must have been Fitzgerald's attraction to an author as thoroughly contemporary as himself and with similar inclinations to self-destruction. Lardner had preceded Fitzgerald in coming into prominence as a popular writer, had an even more provincial background, a much more limited intellectual one, and an unequaled talent for capturing the sound, the feel, the tone of contemporary life. Fitzgerald's admiration and help aside, the relationship must have provoked more hard-headed talk about the craft of writing than Fitzgerald had yet experienced. It was after an evening of drinking with Lardner that he and Fitzgerald tried to pay their respects to Joseph Conrad who was visiting this country and staying on Long Island in the spring of 1923.

Conrad is surely the most important literary influence upon Fitzgerald's work during these years.[3] References to him and his works during the years preceding *The Great Gatsby* become increasingly frequent and important. At the end of *This Side of Paradise,* Amory finds himself at the place Conrad was when he wrote *Almayer's Folly.* In defending his novel to President Hibben in 1920, Fitzgerald said his view of life was the same as the Theodore Dreisers and the Joseph Conrads. In 1922, he called *Nostromo* the greatest novel since *Vanity Fair.* In the same year, he referred to the "great Conradian vitality," and in the next year implied in a book review that Conrad was a greater writer than H. G. Wells. "These enormous and often muddy lakes of sincere and sophisticated observation," as he referred to the kind of novels being written by Dreiser and Wells, will clear the way for "the clear stream" of a Conrad, a Joyce, or an Anatole France.[4] In another review of 1923, Fitzgerald began with a quotation from Conrad's "Youth," calling it "one of the most remarkable passages of English prose written these thirty years."[5] In 1924, an interviewer reported Fitzgerald as saying, ". . . the writer, if he has any aspiration toward art, should try to convey the feel of his scenes, places and people directly—as Conrad does, as a few Americans (notably Willa Cather) are already trying to do."[6]

Finally, the many references to Conrad's work to be found during these years are supported by Fitzgerald's later testimony that he had reread the preface to *The Nigger of the Narcissus* just before writing *The Great Gatsby.*[7] The "magic suggestiveness of music" and the writer's task, "by the power of the written word to make you hear, to make you feel . . . before all, to make you *see,*" were challenges to Fitzgerald's highest ambitions. James Miller summarizes accurately the novel's specific debts to Conrad: "for the use of style or language to reflect theme; for the use of the modified first person narrative; and for the use of deliberate 'confusion' by the re-ordering of the chronology of events."

I *Fitzgerald's Best Novel*

The Great Gatsby is Fitzgerald's best work, his most highly satisfactory novel. In recent years, it has been put forward by many critics as the best novel of Fitzgerald's generation. It has also provoked a ponderous criticism, some as silly as that which connects the two Eggs and Dr. Eckleburg's eyes through a multilingual pun. No novel, however, can be held accountable for the speculations of graduate students mildly deranged during the writing of dissertations. The chief merit of taking the novel seriously has been to help today's readers perceive Fitzgerald's announced intention of writing "something new, something extraordinary and beautiful and simple and intricately patterned."[8]

Though the excellence of *The Great Gatsby* may seem startling when that novel is put beside *This Side of Paradise* and *The Beautiful and Damned*, it seems less startling when we observe how rapidly Fitzgerald developed as a writer and how much writing—and some of it very good writing—he did between 1920 and 1924. The accumulation of experience and feeling, his high aspirations, and his increased awareness of good writing offer further explanation. The material for *The Great Gatsby* is largely material Fitzgerald had used before; at the heart of it once again are the love affairs of Scott Fitzgerald with Ginevra King and Zelda Sayre. Shorn of its climactic events, the novel is the one story Fitzgerald said every writer only tells again and again. The mystery is the way in which all the elements seemed to come together and to say so well what Fitzgerald had to say.

The basic plot of *The Great Gatsby*, like other Fitzgerald plots, develops slowly toward a violently dramatic incident and an ironical conclusion. The story is narrated by Nick Carraway, a Midwesterner recently graduated from Yale, who sells bonds in New York City and rents a house on West Egg, Long Island. His neighbor is Jay Gatsby. Gatsby's dream of reviving the love he once shared with Daisy Fay, now married to Tom Buchanan, is the main thread of the story. Nick's attraction to Jordan Baker, a friend of Daisy's, and Tom Buchanan's affair with Myrtle Wilson, a garage owner's wife, are the parallel plots. The dramatic climax, melodramatic but firmly controlled, is the accidental death of Myrtle Wilson, who is run down by Gatsby's car, driven by Daisy. Tom tells Wilson that Gatsby was driving the car that killed Myrtle, and Wilson walks to Gatsby's estate, kills him and then kills himself. Only Nick and the minister, four or five servants and the postman from West Egg, one casual acquaintance, and Gatsby's father come to the funeral. Tom and Daisy have left New York temporarily, leaving no forwarding address. After the inquest, in which neither Tom's affair with Myrtle nor Daisy's guilt are brought out, Nick leaves for the Midwest, having had enough of the East for a time. The book closes with a prose poem on the eternal attractions and delusions of the romantic vision set against America's romantic expansion from the early Dutch settlement on Long Island to the far Pacific.

II *The Structure of The Great Gatsby*

The Great Gatsby suffers as much as most good novels from having its plot thus extracted and set forth. Directness and simplicity are fundamental characteristics of the novel, but the technique of slowly and enigmatically creating the character of Gatsby, of seeing the novel largely through Carraway's eyes, and of making the most of atmosphere and suggestion make the novel seem longer than its actual length of about fifty thousand words. The story takes place within a single summer, but the chronology does not move straightforwardly along. The first fifty-six pages relate the events of three nights several weeks apart in which Nick Carraway appears at East Egg with his cousin Daisy and Jordan Baker; in New York with Tom Buchanan and Myrtle Wilson; and in West Egg with Jay Gatsby. Immediately after these scenes, Carraway breaks into the narrative to give an account of his ordinary life during and after the events described. The introductory section comes to a kind of climax when Carraway's interest in Jordan Baker leads to two crucial observations: Jordan is "incurably dishonest," and he himself is "one of the few honest people I have ever known."

The next section begins with the Gatsby of parties and rumors. The date, appropriately noted on an old timetable, is July, 1922. The people who come to Gatsby's house are presented in mock-epic fashion. It is the catalogue of ships; the summoning of forces. It even ends with an epic cadence: "All these people came to Gatsby's house in the summer." Carraway, who meets Gatsby, hears from him a history as fantastic in its entirety as the single bit of documentary evidence he offers as proof. The scene at Gatsby's party is parallel with the next scene, a meeting between Nick, Gatsby, and Meyer Wolfsheim, the man who fixed the

1919 World Series. At this point (p. 75), the narrative shifts to Jordan Baker and, through a story she tells to Nick Carraway, back in time to Daisy Fay's house in Louisville in 1917. This was where Jay Gatsby, an obscure second lieutenant, met and fell in love with Daisy. By the end of Chapter Five, then, the reader is able to see the Gatsby of the past and of the present; he still remains something of a mystery, but the forces drawing the various characters together are clearly evident at this point.

Chapter Five, the meeting between Gatsby and Daisy, is at the precise center of the book. The scene is the most static in the novel. It is, by design, timeless. For a moment, after the confusion of the meeting, the rain, and his own doubts, Gatsby holds past and present together. As if to prolong this scene in the reader's mind, Chapter Six leaves the narrative, shifts the scene to the reporter inquiring about Gatsby, and fills in Gatsby's real past. "I take advantage of this short halt," Nick Carraway says, "while Gatsby, so to speak, caught his breath." The deliberate pause illustrates the care with which the novel is constructed. The Gatsby of his self-created present is contrasted with the Gatsby of his real past, and the moment is prolonged before the narrative moves on. The rest of Chapter Six focuses on the first moment of disillusion—Gatsby's peculiar establishment as seen through Daisy's eyes. It ends with Gatsby's central speech: " 'Can't repeat the past?' he cried incredulously. 'Why of course you can!' "

With the beginning of Chapter Seven, the novel gains momentum and the mood changes. The lights in Gatsby's house fail to go on. Heat and sweat become the dominant images. It is as if Fitzgerald were moving the reader from Father Schwartz's early remark in "Absolution" that "When a lot of people get together in the best places things go glimmering," to his later warning: "But don't get up close, because if you do you'll only feel the heat and the sweat and the life." All the climactic events are packed into this chapter, the longest in the book—almost twice as long as any of the others. The prose quickens; events move from the trip to New York and Gatsby's first clash with Tom Buchanan to the accidental death of Myrtle Wilson and the vigil Gatsby keeps outside Daisy's window.

The sustained narrative obviously cannot be pushed much further without a break, and the chapter ends with Gatsby "standing there in the moonlight—watching over nothing." The first part of Chapter Eight pauses while Gatsby and Nick await the events to come. This was the night, Carraway says, that Gatsby told him the story (its factual details have been told earlier in the novel) of his early life. The purpose of the telling here is not to reveal facts but to try to understand the character of Gatsby's passion. The final understanding is reserved for one of those precisely right utterances by which the characters reveal themselves so often in this novel: "In any case," Gatsby says, speaking of Daisy's love for Tom, "it was just personal." The scene ends with Nick pronouncing a kind of benediction over Gatsby as he leaves, "They're a rotten crowd. You're worth the whole damn bunch put together." The resolution comes quickly. The narrator makes a shift in scene, a slight flashback in time, and, as if reported by a detached but on-the-spot observer, Wilson is followed step by step until he finds Gatsby floating on a rubber mattress in his pool and kills him and then himself.

The forward movement of the novel stops there. Chapter Nine is told as it lives in Nick Carraway's memory two years later. The last tales of Gatsby come through Wolfsheim and Mr. Gatz. Like "Benjamin Button," Gatsby's story is a tale of growth to birth. We arrive inexorably in the past—September 12, 1906, to be exact—and read the copy-book maxims of the young James Gatz. The last section pushes Nick Carraway similarly back in time, with that memorable passage about his memories of coming back West from preparatory school. The last page pushes Gatsby, Nick, Daisy—all of us—back into the past. The Dutch sailors' eyes are our eyes, and we are indeed—in the very movement of the novel—"boats against the current, borne back ceaselessly into the past."

This detailed examination of the structure of *The Great Gatsby* calls attention to one of the novel's great virtues: the tight inevitability of its construction. Abstracting from specific details, we see a pattern of movement and withdrawal, and at the center, a moment of dead calm, possession. The scenic character of the first half is heightened by the swiftness of the narrative in the last half. And much of the novel's success in creating a feeling of timelessness despite the story's sharply contemporary events is traceable to the effect of matching the swiftly on-going narrative with a less swift but powerful movement into the past. The image of "the old island that flowered once for Dutch sailors' eyes" has been expertly prepared for, and the story comes to its final line with the inevitability of all high art.[9]

The construction of *The Great Gatsby* is the more remarkable because the crucial ordering of the material did not come until after the book was in galley proof.[10] In its simplest form, the change was that of taking the true story of James Gatz's past out of Chapter Eight and bringing it forward to the beginning of Chapter Six. Thus, as I have noted, the static center of the novel—that moment when Gatsby is alone with Daisy and can hold past and present together—extends itself on into Chapter Seven. The story of the Gatsby who sprang from his Platonic conception of himself is placed precisely where it will make its greatest impact: between that moment of suspended time at the end of Chapter Five and Gatsby's beginning to be aware of the vanity of his own dreams in the party scene of Chapter Six.

That Fitzgerald was consciously striving for this effect is indicated not merely by the transposition of this section but by the very careful and extensive revisions made on almost every page of the galley proofs of these central chapters. The second party, for example, has been changed in many subtle and moving ways. That remarkable image of the motion picture director and his star was originally a part of Gatsby's first party. Fitzgerald apparently recognized its power of "magic suggestiveness" when he removed it there and wrote it into the later scene:

> It was like that. Almost the last thing I remember was standing with Daisy and watching the moving-picture director and his Star. They were still under the white-plum tree and their faces were touching except for a pale, thin ray of moonlight between. It occurred to me that he had been very slowly bending toward her all evening to attain this proximity, and even while I watched I saw him stoop one ultimate degree and kiss at her cheek.[11]

Such a passage is one of dozens which could be cited to illustrate the excellence of Fitzgerald's style, maintained at its highest degree of polish in *The Great Gatsby*. The big changes in the galley proofs are the transposing of materials and the rewriting of scenes involved in that transposition. But throughout the galleys, small changes continually occur to remind us of how Fitzgerald's highly polished style was achieved.

Many of these changes are in individual words: "silhouette" for "shadow," "vanished" for "gone," "soiled" for "spotted," "the blue honey" of the Mediterranean for "fairy blue." A few change the inflections of a speaker's voice: "snapped" instead of "said," cried "ecstatically" instead of "excitedly," "looked at me absently" instead of "replied." Occasionally a better phrase is found: "freedom from money" rather than "spending capacity"; "corky but rather impressive claret" for "wine"; "as if his sturdy physical egotism no longer nourished his peremptory heart" for "as if his sturdy physical egotism wasn't enough for him anymore." A slight change, like having Myrtle Wilson say "had my appendicitis out" rather than "appendix" adds to the delineation of character.

The accumulation of such small changes add up to that Fitzgerald stylistic touch which can only be defined satisfactorily by citing passages. Gatsby's reference to the medal he had received from little Montenegro, for example, was in the galley proof: "Little Montenegro! He lifted up the words and nodded at them—with a faint smile." But when Fitzgerald went over the galleys, he substituted "his" for "a faint" and wrote in that brilliant gloss which now fills out the paragraph: "The smile comprehended Montenegro's troubled history and sympathized with the brave struggles of the Montenegrin people. It appreciated fully the chain of national circumstances which had elicited this tribute from Montenegro's warm little heart."[12]

More often than not in the most heavily revised sections of the galleys, Fitzgerald cut passages, tightened dialogue, and reduced explicit statements in order to heighten the evocative power of his prose. A phase like Gatsby's "I came here to remember, not to forget," is crossed out to let the passage create the attitude rather than have the phrase spell it out. That final remark of Gatsby's had originally followed this speech: " 'I drift here and there trying to forget the sad thing that happened to me.' He hesitated. 'You'll hear about it this afternoon.' "

ACTION IS CHARACTER, Fitzgerald wrote in his notes for *The Last Tycoon*. His galley proof revisions of *The Great Gatsby* reveal his continuing attention to that precept, particularly in his quickening of the dialogue through which the novel often makes its vital disclosures and confrontations. The truth of Gatsby's connection with Oxford was originally revealed to Nick Carraway in a somewhat flat though detailed conversation with Gatsby in which Gatsby tries to define his feeling for Daisy. Most of that conversation was cut out and the Oxford material worked into the taut dialogue between Tom Buchanan and Gatsby in the Plaza Hotel,[13] which prefaces the story's sweep to its final action.

From almost any of Fitzgerald's orginal manuscripts, observations like the above can be multiplied to explain the excellence of his style and how that excellence was achieved. Suffice to say here that these observations on *The Great Gatsby* are all drawn from an examination of changes on the galley proofs; they are the final changes which only came after much previous tuning and blending and refining of that superb instrument which was Fitzgerald's style.

III   *The Truth of the Romantic Vision*

A great deal has been written about the central theme of *The Great Gatsby*, but over and above everything else, it seems to me, is Fitzgerald's attempt to capture the essential truth of the romantic vision. Such truth is ambiguous because the particulars by which it often discloses itself—such as Gatsby's shirts, the green light on the dock, Daisy herself—are far from visionary; in themselves, as often as not, they are false, petty, or meretricious. So, too, Gatsby, who believes in the romantic truth, is often gauche, maudlin, and vulgar. Yet, the vision is not in itself false; and the truth does gleam there at the center, hard and bright and true, an inexhaustible lure to man, an ineradicable part of the vision that gives him his worth.

Trying to illuminate that essential truth is, in the large pattern of the novel, a matter of disposing the characters around Gatsby, who is at the center. Nick Carraway is at the side—too cool, too reasonable, too moral, too much both the realist and the observer ever to do more than touch the center. His honesty, which at most is fidelity to fact, will not permit him to remain there. Jordan Baker, who seems somewhat extraneous to the novel, is a realist of a different kind; "fundamentally dishonest," she is therefore intensely concerned with fact as it can be used to present what she wants it to. She is not dishonest for reason of being possessed with imagination; her dishonesty is rather that which is enslaved to fact and to ego and which denies vision. Tom Buchanan is gross sensuality, a beast lacking in imagination, incapable of clear sight, much less vision. Daisy is the hardest to define. In a sense, she is truth unable to perceive itself, beauty necessarily constrained to take on material form, an ideal consumed in its realization. Thus, the romantic truth is that which arouses awe: "that the rock of the world was founded securely on a fairy's wing," that truth is vision, and that fidelity to it is loneliness, greatness, and terror.

There is much in common between *The Great Gatsby* and *The Heart of Darkness*. The difference may be that Conrad's concern is moralistic; Fitzgerald's, in part at least, aesthetic. Few figures in literature are as alone as Kurtz and Gatsby at the end, both driven there by their faithfulness to a vision: Kurtz, the idealist, losing touch with feeling; Gatsby, the romantic egotist, losing touch with reason. Kurtz and Gatsby arrive at the same end—the horror at the center of truth to any consuming vision. Kurtz is under the moral rod for having kicked himself loose from the universe; Gatsby is chastised by beauty herself for having been consumed by his infatuation.

Nick Carraway's position as narrator and point-of-view character and the breaking up of the chronology of narration are two other similarities with Conrad's work. Like Marlow, Carraway claims to be the completely honest man; and as in *The Heart of Darkness*, in *The Great Gatsby* he violates his code for reasons that bear upon the central theme. Nick lies twice, once to Tom Buchanan when Tom charges Gatsby with being a bootlegger (Nick surely knows), and once again to Tom when Nick has the chance to tell him that Daisy was driving the car that struck Myrtle Wilson. The point is not so forcefully made as is Marlow's deliberate lie to Kurtz's fiancée, but it may be a more subtle point. Obviously, Nick denies what he knows to be true, in the first instance, in defense of Gatsby. Scrupulously honest as he claims to be, he already prefers to side with the gaudy fantasy of Gatsby against the crude truth of Tom Buchanan. The second instance, coming as it does at the end of the story, is an acceptance of the futility of truth in the face of grossness, here displayed as Tom's maudlin sentimentality: "When I saw that damn box of dog biscuits sitting there on the sideboard, I sat down and cried like a baby." Both points heighten Carraway's role as the man in between, faithful to the superiority of what Gatsby represents if incapable of being like Gatsby, and ultimately repelled by the Buchanans.

The morality in *The Great Gatsby* is old-fashioned—provincial squeamishness, Nick calls it. It is a morality based upon spirit over matter, faith over reason, feeling over intellect, and with a kind of Augustinian strain that any beauty short of celestial is likely to draw men into the center where the heat and sweat are. Fitzgerald's attitude toward beauty oftentimes seems moralistic; corruption dwells with beauty; evil hides itself there. The equation of beauty with sin appears in many stories.

Another of the large meanings to be found in the novel is the contrast between the American East and West. This subject has been well explored in Robert Ornstein's "Fitzgerald's Fable of East and West," (*College English* [December, 1956]). Briefly stated, Fitzgerald's "fable" contrasts America's romantic Western past with her unromantic Eastern present. Both Nick Carraway and Jay Gatsby are Westerners, the one from Minnesota, the other from North Dakota. Both are uncomfortable in the East. Both live on West Egg, the unfashionable section of Long Island, just as the Buchanans live on East Egg. Nick returns to the West when the novel is over, and the author concludes with an image of the settlers on Long Island when "man must have held his breath in the presence of this continent, compelled into an aesthetic contemplation he neither understood nor desired, face to face for. the last time in history with something commensurate to his capacity for wonder."

The story of Gatsby himself becomes the story of Western energies which at one time went into settling the continent; at the time of Dan Cody, into exploiting it; and, at Gatsby's time, into illicit activities in the East on the one hand and vain pursuit of an ideal on the other. For Gatsby, the frontier is closed, and the frontier virtues are not adequate for the civilized world in which he has to pursue his dream. The East in which the story takes place is that of "the city seen for the first time, in its first wild promise of all the mystery and the beauty in the world." But this is the city at a distance, as seen from the Queensboro Bridge. It is also the city that lies "west" of the ash heaps of Long Island. Up close, the city is pretty much the "unreal city" of Baudelaire and Eliot. The sordid meetings between Tom and Myrtle and the ugly confrontation between Tom and Gatsby both take place in the city. And, entering or leaving the city, one cannot escape the valley of ashes and the eyes of Doctor T. J. Eckleburg. George B. Wilson lives on the ash heaps, and at the end, too late, even he envisions getting a fresh start in the West.

The theme and attitude are familiar ones in American writing of the early twentieth century. The loss of a rural paradise haunts many writers—even those, like Sinclair Lewis, who ostensibly sneered at the provinces. Fitzgerald's attitude makes *The Great Gatsby* almost a fictional counterpart of Frederick Jackson

Turner's *The Frontier in American History*. Being deprived of that edge of the frontier against which energies, ambitions, ideals, can be freshly honed, the American character must undergo change. The virtues of small-town Christian morality—which appear strikingly in Howells' work—are the kind of measuring rod by which Nick Carraway not only judges but withholds judgment. The myth of the second chance which misleads both Gatsby and Carraway grows out of the common Western experience of pulling stakes one place and trying it again further West. Finally, success, seen in terms of the acquisition of tangible goods, comes to Dan Cody (and to Tom Buchanan's family) from the application of raw energies to the wresting of raw materials from the American earth. At an earlier day, we suppose, Gatsby might have been just such a man, "the pioneer debauchee," as grossly materialistic as the immediate transmutation of base metal into negotiable wealth was likely to make a man, and having that, neither needing nor capable of visualizing the tinsely dream that was Daisy. He is hardly better off as we see him: his vision creates both the mythic past and the orgiastic future; the present time has sullied the one and the other is always just beyond reach.

The American dream and the American disillusion come together in *The Great Gatsby*. The image of the Western past is the green past; the image of the ash heaps, the contemporary wasteland. Tom Buchanan and Daisy are both provincials and both have come East, he vowing to stick it out. Both are careless and corrupt, two qualities for which modern America has been condemned by a succession of writers from the close of the century on. So strong is Nick's reaction to both the dream and the disillusion that he cannot separate Jordan Baker from the society which infects her. He can only leave her behind and go his way alone to the West.

These considerations of larger meaning in the novel set aside the particulars of character, scene, and action. It is, however, only because of the excellence of the particulars that general meanings suggest themselves. The novel is as brilliant in its characterizations, in its individual scenes and its dialogue as in its general effects. We could restrict its scope to that of the novel of manners and still find the novel an admirable achievement. The characters are constantly measuring themselves or inviting us to measure them on a scale of social values. In one scene, for example, Tom Buchanan, the person with highest social position, fulminates against the colored races; yet he defers to Myrtle Wilson, the garage owner's wife, who, in turn, sneers at the bellboy bringing the ice. Farther down the social scale, Mrs. McKee speaks disparagingly of the "Kike" who is far below her. The carefully maintained distinctions between the people of West Egg and East Egg and between the aristocracy living on family money and those who have money still stained, so to speak, by the sweat of their own efforts, are other aspects of the book as the novel of manners. The treatment of society is ironical throughout—the basic irony is that of the "great" in the book's title. The character of Nick Carraway permits a consistent, ironic, point of view that keeps the author from being deluded by the glitter he creates.

The final observation concerns the various excellences which keep the novel fresh through many rereadings. Characterization is, without exception, brilliant. Tom Buchanan, in the description of his physical strength, his past history, his arrogance and his uncertainty, his sensuality and his prudishness, is exactly right. Daisy is probably the weakest of the main characters, perhaps because so much is asked of her in the general pattern of the novel. The minor characters are struck off with that terse exactness which is apparent in much of Fitzgerald's work. Mr. Chester McKee, for example, emerges fully created in the mere fact that he had photographed his wife 127 times since they were married, as does the man in Gatsby's library, who discovers the books are real but the pages uncut. Individual scenes similarly create character, fix moods, or shape attitudes. Tom's buying the dog for Myrtle, the man sent by Gatsby to cut Carraway's grass in the rain, Meyer Wolfsheim displaying his cufflinks, the director all through the second of Gatsby's parties slowly inclining to kiss the cheek of the actress, "a gorgeous, scarcely human orchid of a woman"—all are examples of such scenes.

The character of Nick Carraway is one of the book's triumphs. The somewhat shifting character of Gatsby is kept stable by the firmness of Carraway's characterization, and it is almost always through or in relation to Carraway that we learn of Gatsby. Because of the solidity of Nick's character, Gatsby is able to stand as a character very shadowily created and to gain from that very lack of specification. In all of Fitzgerald's novels, the central male character is designed to impress the reader as possessing qualities superior to those actually displayed in the novel. The failure of both Anthony Patch and Dick Diver is authentically moving to the reader only if he really believes that something extraordinarily fine has disappeared in them and from life. Amory Blaine is a "radiant boy"; but, when the radiance is not shining, he is often merely silly. Only in Gatsby, even in his gorgeous pink rag of a suit, does Fitzgerald succeed in creating a hero whose death, mean as it is, affects a reader in a tragic way. The reason is, in part, that Gatsby is not created so much as a real person but as a mythical one; what he is never emerges clearly and forcefully enough to distract the reader from what he stands for. As Carraway himself sees him, so do the readers: as a person "of some undefined consequence," even though he may simply be the proprietor of an elaborate road-house next door.

Finally, the skill with which Fitzgerald handles violence in the novel is remarkable. Tom's brutality to Myrtle is the first example: "Making a short deft movement, Tom Buchanan broke her nose with his open hand." Myrtle's death and the killing of Gatsby are the other examples, both taking place off-stage, so to speak, and both described tersely and powerfully. Smacking as it does of contrivance, Myrtle's death has to be done so surely and with such impact that the reader will grant Fitzgerald his contrivance and be moved to accept Gatsby's death without cavilling. Language could be employed no more skillfully than Fitzgerald does in ending that scene: "they saw that her left breast was swinging loose like a flap, and there was no need to listen for the heart beneath. The mouth was wide open and ripped at the corners, as though she had choked a little in giving up the tremendous vitality she had stored so long."[14]

IV   *Early Fiction and The Great Gatsby*

Though the total effect of *The Great Gatsby* raises it above Fitzgerald's earlier work, many traces of the early work are to be found in the novel. The details of Gatsby's and Daisy's love affair all come from Fitzgerald's own experiences—already used in *This Side of Paradise, The Beautiful and Damned* (Anthony's affair with Dorothy Raycroft), and in "The Sensible Thing." The New York that both fascinated and repelled Nick Carraway is to be found in "May Day"; Gatsby's early history in "Absolution"; and a short version of the entire novel in "Winter Dreams." A *Saturday Evening Post* story of 1924, "John Jackson's Arcady," is about a man's attempt to recapture his romantic past. When he and his childhood sweetheart meet again and vow their past and present love, the narrator writes: "He felt that he had established dominance over time itself, so that it rolled away from him, yielding up one vanished springtime after another to the mastery of his overwhelming passion." The whole passage which follows strongly suggests *The Great Gatsby*.

Even in small details, the novel often seems to put to real use that which had appeared before. The Long Island scene had been used for finger exercises in a number of articles and short stories written in 1923-24. Oxford and its attractions were previously mentioned in *This Side of Paradise*. The growth of Amory from a personality to a personage, urged seriously but in an amateurish way there, is still in mind when Fitzgerald describes how the "vague contour of Jay Gatsby had filled out to the substantiality of a man." Anthony Patch's fight for his inheritance has a distant kinship with the fact that Gatsby too had received a legacy but lost it in some legal technicality. Citing such connections does not detract from the singularity of the achievement in *The Great Gatsby*, but makes the novel seem less like an isolated masterpiece springing unaccountably into existence.

Just when *The Great Gatsby* was begun is difficult to determine. *The Vegetable*, which was Fitzgerald's major writing task in the winter and spring of 1922-23, could hardly have occupied him to the exclusion of other work. He makes mention of working on a novel during these same months; he seems to have turned to it again during the summer and then, with the excitement of getting his play on stage, to have dropped it. "Scott has started a new novel," Zelda wrote in July, 1923, "and retired into strict seclusion and celibacy." A letter to Maxwell Perkins in mid-October, 1923, tells of putting aside the novel, probably because Fitzgerald found himself $5000 in debt and was uncertain about the prospects of *The Vegetable*. After the play failed in November, the succeeding months were confined—as we have noted—to writing magazine articles and stories. The work he had done on *The Great Gatsby* before he left for Europe—April, 1924—helped him to focus his intentions, but not all of it was usable in the novel his mind was now turning toward.

V   *Response to The Great Gatsby*

The Fitzgeralds were not established at St. Raphaël until June, but they settled on the Riviera in the off-season largely because it promised a cheap and isolated place to work steadily on the novel. By November, despite the first serious rift with Zelda over her infatuation for a French aviator, Fitzgerald was able to send the manuscript of *The Great Gatsby* to Scribner's. It was apparently a completed, polished manuscript, although Fitzgerald continued to send in revisions and made major changes in the structure after the manuscript was set in type.

The response to *The Great Gatsby* at the time of its publication was a mixed one. Gilbert Seldes, who reviewed the book in terms of highest praise for *The Dial*, noted that the press had not been enthusiastic about the novel. Indeed, the reviews which reached the widest audience were mostly unfavorable. The *New York Times* reviewer found the book "curious, mystical, glamorous"; and, for reasons hard to find in the novel, he called the review, "Scott Fitzgerald Looks into Middle Age." The *Herald Tribune* called it "negligible," "uncurbed melodrama," "a tragedy with the flavor of skim milk." In the literary journals and from the best critics *The Great Gatsby* received its due, but even Mencken's praise was strongly qualified.

To Fitzgerald, both the reviews and the sales must have been disappointing. Though the novel was taken seriously as the earlier ones had not been, the sales were mediocre. A year after its publication, it had not sold thirty thousand copies. At the other extreme, the novel had provoked high praise not only from discerning critics but from Edith Wharton, Willa Cather, and T. S. Eliot. Probably even that did not seem enough. From the time he wrote to Edmund Wilson in October, 1924—"My book is wonderful," to a later letter to John Peale Bishop, "The novel I'm sure of. It's marvellous"—Fitzgerald had a sure feeling that he was writing something extraordinary. He was still naïve enough and hopeful enough to assume that a very good novel would sell better than a competent or mediocre one. The August after its publication, in another letter to Bishop, he thanked him for his discerning letter about the book: "It is about the only criticism that the book has had which has been intelligible, save a letter from Mrs. Wharton." "Of all the reviews, even the most enthusiastic," he wrote to Edmund Wilson, "not one had the slightest idea what the book was about."

In the long run, the fact that it made so little money may have been more consequential to Fitzgerald than that it was not adequately understood. Obviously, the Fitzgeralds should have been able to live on $36,000 a year, or on $26,000 or $16,000 for that matter. His total income from 1920 through 1926 was about

$130,000, almost $22,000 a year. But his income from his novels alone was considerably less. By the end of 1926, the three novels together had made less than $40,000 (excluding sales of movie and stage rights) and a negligible continuing sale would have added little more in the years to come. If, at any point in his career, Fitzgerald had chosen to confine his energies to the novel, he would have had to be a far better manager of his finances than he seemed capable of being.

In any consideration of Fitzgerald's use of his talent, his inability to manage money is a central fact. Financial instability is, however, only one aspect of a larger recklessness that cannot be extracted from Fitzgerald's character without destroying his accomplishments as well as modifying his failures. Disappointed as he undoubtedly was by the direct sales of the novel, he soon had the satisfaction of having it taken up by the stage and the movies. The $35,000 he received from both sources certainly removed immediate financial pressures. He responded by producing little writing in 1926 (only five pieces appeared in magazines in 1927), though he did try to get started on a new novel. He had an idea for one sufficiently in mind to call it to Maxwell Perkins' attention by August, 1925, and the idea stayed firmly in his mind throughout that year and the next. Not very much got into finished form, apparently, for when he finally abandoned the idea, salvaging some of it for *Tender Is the Night,* he had completed about twenty thousand words—a poor showing for three years of effort for writers of much less gift than Fitzgerald.

The truth about the twenty months in Europe following the publication of *The Great Gatsby* lies in Fitzgerald's terse description of the summer of 1925: "1000 parties and no work." The closest he came to describing his own malaise is in "The Rich Boy," done between April and August, 1925, and the best piece of writing he was to do for the next two years: "There were so many friends in Anson's life—scarcely one for whom he had not done some unusual kindness and scarcely one whom he did not occasionally embarrass by his bursts of rough conversation or his habit of getting drunk whenever and however he liked." Drinking in 1926 and 1927 was long past being either social custom or a bad joke. "I'm very glad to meet you sir," Fitzgerald is reported as saying in 1927. "You know I'm an alcoholic." Excessive drinking was wrecking him for short periods and long, not only as a writer but as a social being. "Then I was drunk for many years," he wrote in his notebooks, "and then I died."

That most frightening scene in *Tender Is the Night*, the brutal beating Dick Diver suffers in Rome, was transcribed from a drunken fight with a taxi driver in Rome in 1924. This was the same period in which he wrote to John Peale Bishop, "Zelda and I sometimes indulge in terrible four day rows that always start with a drinking party but we're still enormously in love and about the only truly happily married people I know."[15] After the publication of *The Great Gatsby*, the Fitzgeralds continued to live abroad—in Paris and Cap d'Antibes for the remainder of 1925; in the Pyrenees, Paris, Juan-les-Pins during 1926. They returned to America in December, 1926.

VI *All The Sad Young Men*

Fitzgerald's third collection of short stories, *All the Sad Young Men*, was put together in the months after the publication of *The Great Gatsby* and was published in February, 1926. Despite the presence of three of Fitzgerald's best stories, the collection is disappointing chiefly because he had more stories to choose from than for either of the previous collections, and even then some very bad stories are included. Only nine stories are in the collection, but only the best, "The Rich Boy," "Winter Dreams," and "Absolution," seem worth including. All the rest are contrived magazine fiction—"cheap and without the spontaneity of my first work," to use Fitzgerald's own description. The cheapness is only partially masked by paragraphs of effective writing, and it is often worsened by triteness or sentimentality.

The badness of such stories as "Hot and Cold Blood" and "Gretchen's Forty Winks" begins to raise the serious question of what the effect of such deliberately false work is going to be upon Fitzgerald's serious writing. Fitzgerald never wrote a worse scene or created a falser situation than the one in "Hot and Cold Blood" in which the hero refuses to give up his streetcar seat for a woman who turns out to be his pregnant wife. Nor is the essentially hollow quality in "Gretchen's Forty Winks" and "The Sensible Thing" less objectionable because both stories are interesting commentaries on significant experiences in Fitzgerald's life.

"The Sensible Thing" is the fictional counterpart of the article Fitzgerald wrote for the *Post*—"Who's Who—and Why"—describing his early success. George O'Kelly, the hero, is a construction engineer rather than a writer, but he succeeds just as suddenly, in the bush of Peru, by being the man to take over the project when the chief engineer dies. Before this sudden change of fortune, he was an honor graduate from Massachusetts Institute of Technology who had fallen in love with "a dark little girl" he had met while on a construction job in Tennessee. When the story begins, he has come back to New York from that job and is unable to find any better employment than that of a $40-a-week clerk in an insurance firm. O'Kelly's misery in New York, the girl's "nervousness" in Tennessee, his trips to see her, and their break-up draw directly upon Fitzgerald's experience. His triumphant return—bronzed, assured, a success—to win the girl but not to recapture the precious feeling of their first love, concludes the story.

"Gretchen's Forty Winks" draws less directly upon experience, but it still uses a situation patterned upon Fitzgerald's early success. This time, the couple is married. The young man, Roger Halsey, is trying to establish an advertising agency and needs "six weeks that'll decide whether we're going on forever in this rotten little house in this rotten little suburban town." If the layouts he is working on get the big account, his fortune is made. While he's working, his young wife must somehow be kept from growing restless. The situation is complicated by the appearance of George Tomkins, whose successful, orderly, but uncreative life is contrasted with the still-promising, overstrained, creative life of Roger. Roger succeeds in finishing the sketches *and* in keeping Gretchen by putting her to sleep and taking away her shoes.

"Rags Martin-Jones and the Pr-nce of W-les" is a better story than the three just mentioned; but, considering that it is the third story to use the same framework, it should be. "Myra Meets His Family" (1919) and "The Off-Shore Pirate" (1920) are the earlier tales. The pageant created by the hero in this story is designed to win Rags Martin-Jones, the ineffable girl—a girl so rich that all experience bores her. The characters are amusing, the pageant is admirably created (it involves a night club, gangsters, police officers, intrigue, and gunplay), but the story has the air of having been rehearsed too often.

"The Adjuster" and "The Baby Party" come closest to the best stories in this collection, but neither is very close. Both were published in magazines in 1925, both drew upon Fitzgerald's early married experience, and both involve couples with one small child. "The Baby Party" begins as farce, engages itself in reality, and, unfortunately, ends sentimentally. The amusing quarrel which breaks out at a party for Baby Ede becomes a family altercation between the Androses and the Markeys. The description is vivid; the fight between John Andros and Joe Markey is effectively done. The relationships between the two husbands and their wives and between parents and child are illuminated by Fitzgerald's fresh and precise perceptions, but the story's total impression is slight.

"The Adjuster" is a serious story in which a typically sophisticated Fitzgerald woman, ill-suited to her marriage, to domestic life, and to rearing a child, is forced by circumstance to abandon her desire for a divorce and become wife, nurse, and mother. Both of the couples in these stories are in their mid-thirties and have difficulty in reconciling themselves to being the parents that their consciences say they should be. Of most interest in "The Adjuster" is Dr. Moon, a figure by turns realistic and fantastic who is "the adjuster" of the title. He or his presence effects the redemption of the selfish wife by holding her to her obligation through her husband's nervous collapse, through the death of her first child, and through her repeated desires to walk out.

The stories just noted are among Fitzgerald's weaker stories, just as the three best in *All the Sad Young Men* are among the better ones in all his short fiction. "Winter Dreams" is, as Fitzgerald noted, a short version of *The Great Gatsby*, without the melodrama which brings Gatsby to his tragic end. Much of the feeling for locale which so intensifies "The Ice Palace" permeates this story. Fitzgerald's deepest feelings about his status, his desires, his hunger for love and for worldly success, are also well set forth. The story has been discussed in Chapter I, and I add here only an observation about the difference between "Winter Dreams" and *The Great Gatsby*. Without Nick Carraway to give meaning to Gatsby's character, the finely controlled and essentially tragic ending of the novel would probably not come off. Lacking that, and the attitude and skill which created it, the same story in "Winter Dreams" ends far short of tragedy and even of resolution. Fitzgerald in his best work does not often evade; in work below that level he often chooses to mask an evasion in a burst of poetic prose. In "Winter Dreams" there is the burst of Sherwood Anderson rhetoric at the end: "Long ago," he said, "long ago, there was something in me, but now that thing is gone. Now that thing is gone, that thing is gone. I cannot cry. I cannot care. That thing will come no more."

"Absolution" has been mentioned previously as the story which provides a background for Jay Gatsby and as the most explicitly Catholic story in Fitzgerald's work. As has been mentioned before, the story, for all its excellence, is more derivative from naturalistic fiction of the early twentieth century than any other Fitzgerald story. Despite the desires on the part of some readers for more information about Gatsby's past, Fitzgerald's instincts were right in leaving him shadowy. Understatement, suggestion, and mystery do more for his character in the novel than the explicit details do for Rudolph Miller's character in "Absolution." The best part of "Absolution" is the last scene between Father Schwartz and the boy, in which the connection with Gatsby is stronger in tone and in imagery than the more explicit connections of place and time earlier in the story.

"The Rich Boy," one of Fitzgerald's very long short stories, was originally published in two installments in *Red Book* in January and February, 1926. It is a well-known story, closely identified with Fitzgerald's fascination with money. "Let me tell you about the very rich," the narrator says. "They are different from you and me." It was this line which supposedly provoked Hemingway's blunt reply, "Yes, they have more money."

The story follows Anson Hunter from childhood, through Yale and World War I, through one real love affair which breaks off short of realization, and one abortive affair with a girl he doesn't love. Toward the end of the story he has a chance meeting with Paula Legendre, the girl he loved most, and he suffers the torments of the bachelor friend permitted to gaze upon another's domestic bliss. At the close, still a bachelor, Anson goes overseas. He is preoccupied with being thirty, devoid of emotion except when drinking, and then inclined to seek someone to love him, "responding to him like filings to a magnet, helping him to explain himself, promising him something." As a portrait of a rich man, Anson Hunter is more convincingly drawn than Anthony Patch, but he still is patently modeled upon F. Scott Fitzgerald. Anson's love affairs, central to the story, have little to do with his money, and a great deal to do with Fitzgerald's romantic longings. And what Fitzgerald sees in Anson is probably not so much what is characteristic of the rich as what is characteristic of Fitzgerald when he insisted upon living like the rich. The insistent need for assurance of superiority does not strike us as the quality likely to be foremost in a man whose being is solidly based upon fifteen million dollars; rather it is a characteristic of a man who has come into money through his continuing efforts and who has had to convince himself of its reality, as well as of his right to possess it.

"The Rich Boy" and, to a lesser degree, "Absolution," show a control of material and a more fully developed understanding of that material than do the earlier stories. "Winter Dreams" does not quite know how to close out the loss of youth and illusions. It hints at almost everything that Fitzgerald was to define more carefully in the relationship between Daisy and Gatsby. "Absolution," too, is closely related to that central achievement of Fitzgerald's career but, as in "Winter Dreams," intense seriousness still has a way of depending upon borrowed effects, and the author often seems to be urging more for the character and situation than they warrant. "The Rich Boy" achieves, and over longer space, a more consistent tone—one of the marked achievements of *The Great Gatsby*. The attitude toward Anson Hunter hardly varies, and the story ends on the same dispassionate tone with which it began. Though the narrator in that story remains anonymous, he moves into certain sections of the story as strongly as Nick Carraway moved into *The Great Gatsby*. The closing section of "The Rich Boy," seen explicitly through the narrator's eyes, has almost the precise quality that Carraway's presence and reflections give to the novel.

With the publication of *All the Sad Young Men*, Fitzgerald's books were at an end until the appearance of *Tender Is the Night*, eight years later. As could be expected of a writer creating his work so directly out of his life and feelings, the titles of his books are peculiarly fitting to his experiences. *All the Sad Young Men* captures in a phrase the feeling that Fitzgerald had of losing the most vibrant experiences of life even before age took them away. The next chapter recounts briefly a life that became increasingly sad from 1926 to 1934; the following chapter is an account of the short fiction and articles written during that period.

CHAPTER 6

"The Carnival by the Sea"

WHEN the primary objects of love and money could be taken for granted and a shaky eminence had lost its fascination," Fitzgerald wrote at the conclusion of "Early Success," "I had fair years to waste, years that I can't honestly regret, in seeking the eternal Carnival by the Sea."[1] From May, 1924, to December, 1931, the Fitzgeralds spent five years abroad—two extended periods of over two years each, and one summer in between in the year 1928. The events of these years are not happy ones to recount. For despite the indisputable fact that the French Riviera is one of the beautiful spots on earth, the years the Fitzgeralds spent there are marked with ugliness, sterility, and finally insanity. They were, for Fitzgerald, years which left him desolated in the 1930's and made much of his later life an attempt to put back together in any serviceable form an existence that had once gone glittering.

Aside from the publication of *The Great Gatsby* and the work that went into it, the incident of most literary consequence during his first stay abroad was his meeting with Ernest Hemingway. Their friendship was not without strain, but it was a lasting one. Fitzgerald called Hemingway his "artistic conscience," and the two exchanged conversations and letters about their work throughout the 1920's and 1930's. Initially, Fitzgerald was the established writer giving a hand up to a young unknown. Hardly five years later, Fitzgerald was looking at himself as a spent talent, while Hemingway's *Farewell to Arms* was selling ninety-three thousand copies the first year.

Fitzgerald may have known of Hemingway's work before he went abroad in 1924; certainly he heard of him during the months he was bringing *The Great Gatsby* into publication. He wrote Edmund Wilson shortly after the novel was published that he had looked up Hemingway, who was taking him to see Gertrude

Stein. During that summer of 1925, he was seeing a good deal
of him in Paris. Almost from the beginning of their acquaintance,
he began trying, sometimes with Hemingway's knowledge, sometimes without, to get Hemingway recognized. Glenway Wescott
recalled in 1941 how Fitzgerald had taken him aside in this
earlier time and had discussed ways of getting "the one true
genius" of the 1920's recognized.[2] Fitzgerald's strong personal
interest found its way into an article, "How to Waste Material,"
published in *The Bookman* in May, 1926.[3]

The essay began as an attack on the dominant literary compulsion of the 1920's: to write "significantly" about America.
By that route Fitzgerald arrived at a discerning review of Hemingway's *In Our Time* (1925) as the book of an author who had
profited from recent American fiction's "dismal record of high
hope and stale failure." He singled out "Big Two-Hearted River"
as one of the best contemporary short stories. Only Gertrude
Stein's "Melanctha," Lardner's "Golden Honeymoon," and Anderson's "The Egg" had impressed him as much. "I read it with the
most breathless unwilling interest I have experienced since
Conrad first bent my reluctant eyes upon the sea."

His judgment of other stories in the Hemingway collection is
sound; his observations accurate. "My Old Man" is singled out
as the least successful story, partly because "there is an echo
of Anderson's way of thinking in those sentimental 'horse stories,'
which inaugurated his respectability and also his decline four
years ago." He notices the way Nick's feelings illuminate the
stories, the absence of exposition without a loss of impact, the
power of the interpolated sketches. He concludes by saying,
"many of us . . . have felt a sort of renewal of excitement at these
stories wherein Ernest Hemingway turns a corner into the street."

Fitzgerald was instrumental in convincing Hemingway to go
with Scribner's, for he put Hemingway into correspondence with
Maxwell Perkins. He shared with Hemingway the feeling toward
Sherwood Anderson which provoked *Torrents of Spring*, the
parody of Anderson which freed Hemingway from his contract with Boni and Liveright. When Hemingway did sign
with Scribner's, it was partly because, as he wrote to Fitzgerald,
"I would like to be lined up with you."

In August, 1925, when Hemingway visited the Fitzgeralds on
the Riviera, he brought with him a copy of *The Sun Also Rises*.
He later revised the novel as a result of Fitzgerald's criticisms.
At the same time, Fitzgerald told Hemingway something of his

plans for his next novel, "The World's Fair." Their exchanges
in the years following range from peevish responses to imagined
injuries to broad joking about each other's work. The decline
of their close relationship in the later 1920's and 1930's may have
been due to Fitzgerald's feeling which he once recorded: "I talk
with the authority of failure—Ernest speaks with the authority
of success." "With Ernest," he wrote to Edmund Wilson in
1933, "I seem to have reached a state where when we drink
together I half bait, half truckle to him."

The fault, however, was far from being Fitzgerald's alone.
However insulting he may have been in conversation, Fitzgerald
never abused him publicly as Hemingway was to do in "The
Snows of Kilimanjaro," where the has-been writer is not only
F. Scott Fitzgerald in fact, but in name, in that story's original
appearance in *Esquire*. Their friendship did not break completely
as a result of the story, but only perhaps because it had been
gradually thinning out in the late 1920's and early 1930's.

Hemingway was only one of a great many artistic people
the Fitzgeralds came to know in the last half of the 1920's.
Like other members of the international set, they shifted res-
idences from Paris to the Riviera, but they made staying on the
Riviera in the off-season one of their distinctions. During their
first stay, they went as far south as Rome and Capri. During
their last, they found themselves in Switzerland where Zelda
was treated after her first major breakdown. Most of the time
was spent between Cannes and Nice, the scene described with
such evocative power in the beginning of *Tender Is the Night*
and in Zelda Fitzgerald's novel, *Save Me the Waltz*. In many
ways, Zelda's volatile, undisciplined prose creates the most
striking impression of these years abroad.

As with most other experiences of Fitzgerald's life, the events
of these years found their way into fiction and nonfiction. The
Post article (1924) "How to Live on Practically Nothing a Year"
is faithful to the first trip abroad and their stay in the "hot,
sweet south of France" in the off-season. "The Rough Crossing,"
another *Post* story (1929), describes their third trip. "Show Mr.
and Mrs. F. to Number ——," by both Scott and Zelda, in *Esquire*
(1934), is a kaleidoscope of all the years up to 1934—just as
"Auction—Model 1934" describes their lives through the accumu-
lations of their past travels. From 1926 to 1934, a great number
of stories and articles were created out of one incident or another from their trips abroad.

"There was no one at Antibes this summer," Fitzgerald wrote John Peale Bishop in 1925, "except me, Zelda, the Valentinos, the Murphy's, Mistinguet, Rex Ingram, Dos Passos, Alice Terry, the MacLeishes, Charles Bracket, Maude Kahn, Esther Murphy, Marguerite Namara, E. Phillips Openheim, Mannes the violinist, Floyd Dell, Max and Chrystal Eastman, ex-Premier Orlando, Etienne de Beaumont—just a real place to rough it and escape from all the world."[4] The list is representative, not inclusive. In a short story, "One Trip Abroad," Fitzgerald describes the kinds of people Nicole and Nelson Kelly went with during their years abroad:

> The first crowd they had known was largely American, salted with Europeans; the second was largely European, peppered with Americans. This latter crowd was 'society,' and here and there it touched the ultimate *milieu*, made up of individuals of high position, of great fortune, very occasionally of genius, and always of power.

"One could get away with more on the summer Riviera," he wrote in "Echoes of the Jazz Age" (1931), "and whatever happened seemed to have something to do with art."

The many anecdotes that emerge from these years have several things in common. Almost all involve the alcoholic haze which hung over much of the rest of Fitzgerald's life. Almost as many involve one or both of them in basically destructive acts or desires. Some are carelessly self-destructive, as their driving their car onto a railroad trestle and going to sleep; others are a courting of purposeless violence, as their threats of sawing a waiter in half. Many disclose an antagonism between the Fitzgeralds which was never so much jealousy as an intense rivalry over their respective talents, ambitions, daring, and imagination. Ominously for a writer, very few of these anecdotes had much to do with Fitzgerald's work, though many found their way into his fiction.

Zelda Fitzgerald's passion to dance was the first certain sign of her mental disorder, though such diverse observers as Ernest Hemingway and Rebecca West had called her "crazy" as early as 1924-25. Fitzgerald later said that he had noticed signs of her coming breakdown in 1927. In October of that year she mentioned to Carl Van Vechten that she had joined the Philadelphia Ballet. Her desire not merely to study ballet but to become a professional dancer—she was twenty-eight—became increasingly obsessive from that year on.

First in America, then in Europe, her single-minded devotion to an impossible goal must have rubbed Fitzgerald's own conscience raw. His inability to finish a novel, to work without drinking, and to drink without remembering the work he was neglecting, was nakedly exposed by Zelda Fitzgerald's intense application. Thus, while she danced, he managed what they had of a domestic establishment, felt himself slipping into the thirties still identified with *This Side of Paradise*, and became increasingly truculent and abusive and incapable of gaining control. "Thirty-two years old," he wrote in his Ledger for 1928, "and sore as hell about it." An additional notation was heavily underscored: "OMINOUS. No Real Progress in ANY way & *wrecked myself with dozens of people.*" The entries for 1928 bear out the caption: "June—Carried home from the Ritz; July—Drinking and general unpleasantness—first trip jail; August—second trip jail—general carelessness and boredom."

Fantastic as Zelda Fitzgerald's ambition was, her dancing career went far enough to give her some hope of a professional engagement. In *Save Me the Waltz*, Alabama Knight makes her professional debut—a successful one—in Rome, but at the same time she incurs a foot infection which closes her career. In Zelda Fitzgerald's life, her dancing career ended in a complete nervous collapse in April, 1930. The specialists at Montreux, Switzerland, where Fitzgerald took her in the summer of 1930, diagnosed her case as schizophrenia. From that time on, she was never able to resume her old life for long; and, from then on, she was Scott Fitzgerald's almost constant care.

During the years abroad, which read like a flutter of travel brochures—Paris, Sorrento, Capri, the Pyrenees, Arles, Algiers, Lausanne, Munich—the Fitzgeralds made three stays in America before returning permanently. The second trip back brought Fitzgerald to Hollywood. In January, 1927, when he was asked to do a college story for Constance Talmadge, he turned out a competent script, a mixture of fantasy and romance, which was never produced. The experience was typical of other frustrating attempts to employ his craft for the movies. While in Hollywood, he met Mary Pickford, John Barrymore, Richard Barthelmess, Lois Moran (who became Rosemary Hoyt in *Tender Is the Night*), and other celebrities; and the life of parties, drinking, and playing pranks went on much as it had done abroad.

Of more importance than the two months spent in Hollywood was the acquiring of a home called Ellerslie outside Wilmington, Delaware. Much of the writing he did during these years was done at Ellerslie either during the first period of residence through 1927 until spring 1928 or during the following winter when the Fitzgeralds came back after a summer abroad. Their lives had evidently slid too far into disorder to be greatly affected by the comparative tranquility of a suburban home. Quarrels were frequent, visitors plentiful, and writing fitfully done and often discouraging. By the time their two-year lease ended in the spring of 1929, Fitzgerald had convinced himself he could not work at Ellerslie and left for Europe again. The third trip to America Scott made alone when his father died in January, 1931, in Rockville, Maryland. Zelda was in the sanitarium and Scottie was left in Paris with a governess.

When he returned, Zelda was sufficiently recovered to travel, and the trips they took to Annecy, Munich, Vienna were, accord- to Zelda, "like the good gone times when we still believed in summer hotels and the philosophies of popular songs. Another night we danced a Wiener waltz, and just simply swep' around."[5] Fitzgerald, too, seemed to have felt the charm of this period. He called the "nine months before her second breakdown"—the summer in Europe, the fall with Zelda in Montgomery and Scott in Hollywood—the happiest of their lives.

In September, 1931, they sailed for America, leaving Europe permanently behind. Judge Sayre died shortly after their return, and Zelda Fitzgerald's second breakdown came at the end of January, 1932. That spring Fitzgerald moved to Baltimore where Zelda had been receiving treatment. They moved into a large house on the Bayard Turnbull estate, where they were to live until the beginning of 1934. His address, as he noted in a letter to Edmund Wilson shortly after they got settled, was "La Paix (My God!)."

CHAPTER 7

Stories and Articles: 1926-34

FROM 1926 to 1934, Fitzgerald published forty-nine stories, the same number included in Ernest Hemingway's major collection. In addition, Fitzgerald published a dozen articles and completed the work that went into *Tender Is the Night*. This is no small amount of writing during a period generally regarded as one of decline. More important, though Fitzgerald and his readers felt disappointed in his not producing a second novel of the stature of *The Great Gatsby*, a surprising amount of good writing appears during these years.

The best sustained stories were those about Basil Duke Lee, discussed in a previous chapter. The eight published stories and an unpublished one deserve a higher place in Fitzgerald's work than they have been given. So regarded, they fill a place in 1928-29 that makes the period between *The Great Gatsby* and *Tender Is the Night* seem less empty than it otherwise appears. They show how professional a writer Fitzgerald was; for, though the first of the stories was done at Ellerslie in a period of comparative peace, the last four were done under the strain of Zelda's dancing mania in Europe in the chaotic summer of 1928 and during a period of quarrels, belligerent despair, and drunkenness back at Ellerslie.

From February, 1926, to June, 1927, Fitzgerald wrote no stories. Part of the time was spent on the novel called, at various times, *The World's Fair*, *The Boy Who Killed His Mother*, and *Our Type*. It was also the period in which the stage success of *The Great Gatsby*—it opened February 2, 1926, and ran three months—and the sale of the movie rights gave him temporary freedom from financial worries. The published output for 1926 after the appearance of "The Rich Boy" in the January and February *Red Book*, was the essay on Hemingway ("How to Waste Material") and two mediocre stories, "The Adolescent Marriage" and "The Dance." The year 1927 was not much better: three *Post* stories, one for *Woman's Home Companion,* and the article "Princeton" for *College Humor.* But then again came a summoning of energy that saw seven good stories published in 1928; eight stories, four of them excellent, in 1929; and eight stories of mixed quality in each of the years 1930, 1931, and 1932. Work on *Tender Is the Night* accounts for the relatively unproductive year of 1933, when he published four stories, the article on Ring Lardner for the *New Republic,* and "One Hundred False Starts" for the *Post.*

The stories of these years include the two groups of Basil and Josephine stories, a large number of stories contrived from familiar Fitzgerald characters and situations, some drawing on current experiences, a number of retrospective ones, and a few like "A Short Trip Home" and "Family in the Wind" that are somewhat uncharacteristic of Fitzgerald's magazine fiction. At least two—"Babylon Revisited" and "Crazy Sunday"—are commonly included among Fitzgerald's best stories. The best of them went into *Taps at Reveille,* making that collection the richest of his short-story collections. A number of others were included in Malcolm Cowley's edition, *The Stories of F. Scott Fitzgerald,* and in Arthur Mizener's edition, *Afternoon of an Author.* About half remain uncollected.

I *The Josephine Stories*

The Josephine stories include "First Blood," "A Nice Quiet Place," "A Woman with a Past," "A Snobbish Story," and "Emotional Bankruptcy." All appeared in the *Post* between April 5, 1930, and August 15, 1931; the first three were reprinted in *Taps at Reveille.* The central character relies heavily upon Fitzgerald's memory of Ginevra King, and the stories themselves are the successors to the Basil Duke Lee series. Josephine carries the burden of the story in the same way that Basil carried the burden of that group. If she is a less successfully created character, as I think she is, it may be because Fitzgerald did not, could not, fully understand her or be as privy to her youthful feelings and experiences as he could with Basil. Mrs. Ginevra King Pirie wrote to Arthur Mizener, in part: "I was too thoughtless in those days & too much in love with love to think of consequences. These things he has emphasized—and over-emphasized in the Josephine stories, but it is only fair to say I asked for some of them."[1]

The statement is accurate, as far as it goes, in defining the fictional character of Josephine. Being in love with love certainly is her outstanding characteristic. In a larger sense, Josephine is Fitzgerald's vision of an ideal woman, but since the ideal is unattainable, he invests the woman he creates with as much of this ideal as will still leave her credible as a person. It is a leading characteristic of Josephine that she, too, responds most readily to the unattainable or unobtainable.

The first of the stories, "First Blood," shows Josephine Perry at sixteen, the daughter of a family well-established in Chicago society and almost very rich. The year is 1914, and she is introduced as an unconscious pioneer of that generation that was destined to get out of hand. The story, like so much of Fitzgerald's work, is both a character study and a plot story. Josephine is shown as determined, conceited, rebellious, indiscreet, and yet very young and innocent. She is chafing under her parents' demand that she stop going somewhere every day. Her response is typical of her—and of Fitzgerald's dialogue: "How crazy! How utterly insane! Father's got to be a maniac I think. Next thing he'll start tearing his hair and thinking he's Napoleon or something."

The plot involves her desire, growing out of her mixed character, to force attention from Anthony Harker, a twenty-two-year-old "happy fellow, lazy, rich enough, pleased with his current popularity." Anthony is engaged to Josephine's sister; although he first treats Josephine's interest in him as that of an infatuated kid, he ends up writing her a four-page letter pledging his undying love. Josephine has what she wants: not Harker himself but the satisfaction of knowing she could have him if she wished.

The short final section of the story, so often a strong part of the Basil stories, is less successful here. Now that she can have him, she no longer wants him. Harker's parents are forced to send him West to forget. Josephine's reflections, both amusing and shallow, are more Fitzgerald's than the character's. The story ends with a mildly amusing irony, as Josephine denies a rumor that she and Travis de Coppet are married. She conceals the fact that they had tried to get married but couldn't find a minister. " 'Oh, how perfectly terrible!' she repeated. 'That's the kind of story that gets started by jealous girls.' "

"A Nice Quiet Place," depends more on plot and less on character than the first Josephine story. It begins with the Fitzgerald flourish that distinguishes so much of his fiction. "All that week she couldn't decide whether she was a lollipop or a roman candle—through her dreams, dreams that promised uninterrupted sleep through many vacation mornings, drove a series of long, incalculable murmurings in tune with the put-put-put of their cut-outs, 'I love you—I love you,' over and over."

The time is early summer, six months after her mother had taken her East to the Brearley School at the end of the previous story. "It was only recently," the author writes, "that gossip had begun to worry Josephine. Her own theory was that, though at thirteen or fourteen she had been 'speedy'—a convenient word that lacked the vulgar implication of 'fast'—she was now trying to do her best, and a difficult enough business it was, without the past being held against her; for the only thing she cared about in the world was being in love and being with the person she currently loved." Beyond this point, a conventional plot takes over.

When Josephine is sent to an out-of-the-way summer vacation spot to reduce her speed somewhat, she meets the fabulous Sonny Dorrance, the most susceptible and desirable man in America. He conceals his identity at their first meeting; but, when she finds out after returning to Lake Forest just who he is, she tricks her parents into banishing her once again from the high life to the pure simple life of Island Farms.

The last of the collected Josephine stories, "A Woman with a Past" finds Josephine exactly seventeen, blasé, and bored. The scene is New Haven; the situation involves Josephine at the Yale prom. The central idea is an effectively made contrast between the ephemeral high-voltage effect of Josephine and the dull but durable power of Adele Craw. Adele, a pretty girl with thick legs, is president of the senior class, forceful, dominant, and without moral blemish. Josephine's attempt to get Adele's fiancé, Dudley Knowleton, almost succeeds but eventually comes to nothing.

Between the two episodes in which she pursues Dudley, Josephine is locked in a room with a sleek Southerner, Book Chaffee. She escapes that scandal, but later she is expelled from Miss Brereton's school in a confusion of supposed misdeeds for which she is not responsible. Meeting Dudley with the Yale baseball team at Hot Springs, she learns that Adele's claim is too strong, her peculiar attractions superior to those of Josephine; for the first time in her life she has tried for a man and failed.

At the end of the story, she lets a Princeton man drop his arm around her yielding shoulder and walk with her out into the spring night.

Like the Basil Duke Lee stories, the Josephine stories show the central character developing over a fairly short but important period of time. Dudley Knowleton is the first man to make Josephine realize that "one couldn't go on forever kissing comparative strangers behind closed doors." Unfortunately, the two remaining stories do not adequately continue the development suggested in "A Woman with a Past."

"A Snobbish Story" is the weakest of the group, weak in a way some other Fitzgerald stories are weak. In trying to invest Josephine with a change in the direction of seriousness, he loses the vitality of his central character. Josephine becomes involved with John Boynton Bailey, who is "extraordinarily handsome" but poor, something of a radical and married. Fitzgerald's intention is to show Josephine's defiance of Chicago society through her interest in John Bailey, but neither the character nor the situation carries much conviction.

The last story, "Emotional Bankruptcy," is a better story quite aside from the interest it provokes as the means of introducing the concept of "emotional bankruptcy" which Fitzgerald felt was so applicable to his own life. At the peak of Josephine's "flowering marvelously day by day into something richer and warmer," she begins to realize that her love affairs are like "a game played with technical mastery, but with the fire and enthusiasm gone." Her ideal man, as she defines him in this story, is not necessarily handsome, but pleasant looking, with a good figure and strong: "Then he'd have to have some kind of position in the world, or else not care whether he had one or not. . . . He'd have to be a leader, . . . and dignified, but very pash, and with lots of experience, so I'd believe everything he said or thought was right."

Such a man seems to be present in Captain Edward Dicer; but, when he kisses Josephine, she feels nothing. As the reader last sees her, her "youthful cockiness" gone, he can hardly fail to be moved by Fitzgerald's peculiar skill of investing his heroes and heroines with momentary but genuine emotional value:

> She was very tired and lay face downward on the couch with that awful, awful realization that all the old things are true; one cannot both spend and have. The love of her life had come

by, and looking in her empty basket, she had found not a flower left for him—not one. After a while, she wept.

"Oh, what have I done to myself?" she wailed. "What have I done?"

II *Representative Magazine Fiction*

Though only about one-third of the stories found their way into collections, there were thirty-three stories—in addition to the thirteen in the Basil and Josephine series—published in the *Post* between 1926 and 1934. Three stories in other popular magazines and one, "Millionaire's Girl," largely Zelda's, were also published in these years.

These stories serve to confirm impressions already established by previous Fitzgerald magazine fiction. All of them are long stories and, at least until those of the middle 1930's, are expertly plotted. The stories they tell are faithful to the illustrations which accompany them: the handsome, well-dressed man; the clinging or pursuing girl; and, somewhere in the background, a rich father or benign employer. Some, like "Jacob's Ladder," create interesting characters and move through multiple complications to a serious, uncontrived ending. Some are variations on previous stories, such as "Your Way and Mine" is on "The Third Casket," or as "Love Boat" is on "John Jackson's Arcady." Some, like "The Swimmers," are serious attempts to encompass a large portion of the lives of the central characters and to relate those lives to larger themes. Stripped of their details, almost all are stories of poor boys falling for rich girls, or of rich men or boys falling for poor girls. Usually, intelligence, imagination, or beauty; hard work, daring, or luck manage to overcome the handicaps of social position.

A number of stories written before 1928 go back into Fitzgerald's Princeton past and into that period in New York just before and after his rise to fame. Two of the early ones, "A Penny Spent" (1925), and "Presumption" (1926), make the most of the young man who wins out through a display of imaginative bravado. Another, "The Bowl," is a serious attempt to examine an undergraduate attitude from the perspective of greater maturity: Dolly Harlan's mixed feelings toward being a football hero. A half-dozen of the stories use Europe for a setting. Most of these, like "Babylon Revisited," were written between 1929 and 1931, Fitzgerald's last long period of residence abroad. Another group of stories, written between 1931 and 1934, have snobbery as a theme; they doubtless reflect Fitzgerald's mood as he sought to find blame for the insecurity of his position as both writer and public figure.

Almost all of the later stories use a Southern setting, usually Maryland or Virginia, and provide Southern backgrounds for the central characters. The movies figure prominently in three stories, hospitals in two; both settings reflect Fitzgerald's life at the time they were written. One story, "A Freeze-Out" (1931) goes back to St. Paul and Fitzgerald's early youth for its setting and situation. Another, "No Flowers," revisits the college prom in the person of a young girl of the 1930's who contrasts her present age of tin with the golden age through which her mother had lived. "New Types," a bad story in its total effect, begins as a serious attempt to describe the new woman Fitzgerald apparently saw developing in the mid-1920's. Finally, the worst of the stories are "plants"—mere plot stories announcing their destination in the first page—that are often either melodramatic of sentimental.

A glance at a few of the representative stories will indicate the kinds of interest these stories still possess. "The Swimmers" makes the most deliberate and effective contrast between Europe and America. Aside from an undergraduate war story, "Sentiment and the Use of Rouge," written entirely from the imagination, Europe does not figure prominently in Fitzgerald's fiction until 1925. The stories written close to that time are contrived plot stories which use Europe for little more than atmosphere. "Love in the Night" (*Post*, 1925), "A Penny Spent" (*Post*, October, 1925), and "Not in the Guidebooks" (*Woman's Home Companion*, November, 1925) are stories of negligible worth. Europe does not appear again as a setting until 1929. A half-dozen European stories, all written between 1929 and 1931, were put into later collections. Of the five others, "The Swimmers" and "A New Leaf" are the most interesting.

In "The Swimmers," Europe is almost as important as the characters. Throughout this account of a Virginia gentleman's unsuccessful marriage to a French wife, the contrasts between Europe and America are as obviously drawn as in a story by Henry James. Indeed, a passage like this one describing "the American girl" could have been taken from a James story: "In her grace, at once exquisite and hardy, she was the perfect type of American girl that makes one wonder if the male is not being sacrificed to it, much as, in the last century, the lower strata in England were sacrificed to produce the governing class."

Though the story ends with a desperate contrivance, it is worth reading if only for its style and for its skillful contrasts between two cultures.

"A New Leaf," which begins in Europe and shifts to America, is of most interest because of its central character, Dick Ragland, whose alcoholic charm is one of many characteristics he shares with Fitzgerald: "'Just when somebody's taken him up and is making a big fuss over him, he pours soup down his hostess' back, kisses the serving maid, and passes out in the dog kennel. But he's done it too often. He's run through about everybody, until there's no one left.'"

The heroine's attempt to mother him into reform fails; and, before the story ends, he jumps overboard to his death. "Isn't life cruel, sometimes—" the girl says, in another transparent reflection of Fitzgerald's own thoughts—"so cruel, never to let anybody off."

A theme that gained much of Fitzgerald's attention in these forgotten stories is that of snobbery. If we include "The Swimmers" and another European story, "Hotel Child," six uncollected stories are preoccupied with snobbery of one kind or another. "Two Wrongs," reprinted in *Taps at Reveille*, is the best of this type. "A Change of Class" (*Post*, 1931), the most obvious and mechanical of the uncollected group, is the story of a barber who moved out of his class and back into it with the ups and downs of the market. "The Rubber Check," about a poor young man who tries to make his way by assuming the manners of the upper class, comes closest to revealing Fitzgerald's own feeling of occupying a social position to which he was not really entitled.

Of the other uncollected stories, "What a Handsome Pair" (*Post*, 1932) is noteworthy because of the skill with which Fitzgerald makes an essentially didactic comment upon the nature of marriage. One marriage succeeds because Theodore Van Beck, a composer, marries an Irish waitress who shares none of his artistic interests but who is content to mother him, love him, and allow him great freedom. The other fails because the girl who turns down Van Beck later marries a man who shares all her interests. The marriage becomes an intense competition which reaches bottom when he is rejected by the army but she is accepted by the Red Cross for a war assignment overseas. "On

Schedule" (*Post*, 1933) is interesting for the amusement Fitzgerald is still able to get out of looking at himself trying to manage his family's life at Ellerslie. The story's central character, Rene du Cary, feels that if everyone will just stay on schedule, he can keep a complicated life running smoothly.

In the last stories of these years, one begins to see signs of Fitzgerald's crack-up. The beginning of "Diagnosis" (*Post*, 1932) is an essay about cracking up, a kind of unpolished, fictional version of the "Crack-Up" essay itself. Similarly, in "The Rubber Check" (August, 1932), Percy Wrackham, a character in the story, is always making up lists—the same lists Fitzgerald ascribes to his own compulsions in "The Crack-Up." "Her Last Case" (*Post*, 1934) is about a thirty-five-year-old Virginian, Ben Dragonet, who has mysteriously aged, lost his health and his peace of mind. When he is not drunk, he walks his nights away, brooding about the past. "Family in the Wind," as Arthur Mizener has pointed out, is an early version of the state of mind Fitzgerald described later in "Pasting It Together."

When Fitzgerald went through the large number of stories published after 1926 to select the contents of *Taps at Reveille*, he first included "A New Leaf" and "Her Last Case." Either story would have been as good a choice as the weaker stories in the volume, though the ending of "Her Last Case" is almost ruinous to the story. Of the rest, only "The Swimmers," "What a Handsome Pair," "On Schedule," and "The Bowl" seem to me to be nearly equal to the stories Fitzgerald did select.

III   *Taps at Reveille*

Of the stories in *Taps at Reveille* which drew upon personal experiences, "Two Wrongs" is the most revealing. Its central actions relate closely to the drunkenness, belligerence, and subsequent guilt of Fitzgerald's life in 1928 and 1929 and to Zelda Fitzgerald's dancing. The hero, Bill McChesney, is a producer rather than a writer—a kind of grown-up Basil Duke Lee—who is still capable of saving a play when the actors threaten to walk out. Almost everything of Fitzgerald's early success is in this story, as are Fitzgerald's later feelings that the late 1920's marked his decline. McChesney is a markedly dual character: on one hand he is "a fresh-faced Irishman exuding aggressiveness and self-confidence"; on the other, "the quietly superior, sensitive one, the patron of the arts, modeled on the intellectuals of the Theatre Guild." Emmy, McChesney's wife, is a Southern girl who decides to become a ballet dancer at twenty-eight. Three years after ·their marriage and after the husband's two flops and a period of increased drinking, McChesney becomes somewhat mildly attracted to Lady Sybil Combrinck. In a climax which exposes most of Fitzgerald's feelings of insecurity and guilt, McChesney crashes Lady Sybil's party and is thrown out. While he goes on to get blind drunk, Emmy has had to arrive at the hospital alone, falls in getting out of the taxi, and delivers a stillborn child. It is after she recovers that she begins to dance.

Despite the melodramatic climax, the story exposes many of Fitzgerald's deep feelings: his real and imagined abuse of Zelda and her abuse of him, his feeling of decline both in popularity and personal strength, his attitude toward his excessive drinking, and his still intense feelings for rank and position. The marital relationship, as it is described in the concluding section of the story, anticipates that of the Divers in *Tender Is the Night*. As Emmy increases in vitality, McChesney declines. He comes "to lean, in a way, on her fine health and vitality," the author comments. When she receives an offer to dance at the Metropolitan, McChesney insists that she take the opportunity. He leaves for the West feeling that the trip is, for him, a definite finish. "He realized perfectly that he had brought all this on himself and that there was some law of compensation involved."

There is nothing new here in Fitzgerald's using the events and feelings of his own life soon after they had taken place, nor in his turning to melodrama and contrivance to enhance the· story. There is, however, something moving about the preciseness of the description and about the feeling of helplessness which pervades the story—"an almost comfortable sensation of being in the hands of something bigger than himself." The reader with a knowledge of Fitzgerald's life may find the story too uncomfortably close to reality to be enjoyed.

"The Bridal Party," written shortly after "Two Wrongs," also uses a recently experienced event for its plot. Arthur Mizener ascribes its central situation to the wedding of Powell Fowler in Paris in the summer of 1930, but he attributes the feeling to Fitzgerald's deepest reactions to his own marriage.[2] The situation dramatized in the story is very close to the central one to which Fitzgerald returned again and again. The rich young man about to be married learns he has lost every cent; but without a moment's hesitation he goes through with every expensive detail of the elaborate wedding. As it turns out, such bravado so confounds adverse Fortune that, ten minutes before the wedding, he is offered a salary of $50,000 a year. This triumph is set against the failure of the other central character, a man too poor, too afraid, too futile to win the girl in the first place, and now come too late into an inheritance of a quarter of a million dollars. Despite his ineffectual attempts to break into the wedding plans, he is forced to admire the superior brashness of his successful rival. Though many Fitzgerald stories create similar figures involved in similar actions, few disclose these two contrasting images—the failure who hesitates, the successful man who always pushes on—as clearly as they are presented here.

"The Rough Crossing," like "One Trip Abroad," is a story about a couple like the Fitzgeralds in Europe during the late 1920's. The first, written a year and a half before the other, is a less ambitious, less successful story; it is little more than the reflection of the jealousies aroused in both the Fitzgeralds by their being attractive to and attracted by other people. The central character is the playwright, Adrian Smith, who, on a trip abroad, is drawn to a young girl half his age. The jealousy of his wife Eva and her own flirtation motivate the action. The storm, during which Eva gets drunk and mistakenly thinks Adrian is with the young girl, is a way of emphasizing the chaos that seems close to the surface of both the main characters' lives. The boat arrives in Europe, the young girl has forgotten that she ever kissed Adrian, and the Smiths ostensibly pick up life at a less stormy level.

"One Trip Abroad," written in 1930, is a more ambitious story and one directly connected with *Tender Is the Night*. Like *Tender Is the Night*, the story is centrally concerned with the gradual decay in Europe of a handsome American couple of good breeding and sufficient wealth to be idle. The structure of the story poses the central couple, Nicole and Nelson Kelly, against an older couple, the Mileses, at the beginning, and against another young couple, who appear at both the beginning and the end. In these couples, the Kellys see themselves as they will become and as they actually are.

As in all the successive versions of *Tender Is the Night*, the corruption of innocence is a central theme. Almost all the important parts of the final version of the novel are in "One Trip Abroad": the ease and grace and brilliance of the Kellys; the glit-

tering surface of their lives which conceals the growing empti-
ness within; the cynicism and waste in Oscar Dane (Abe North in
the novel); the steady drinking amidst the international set; the
violence into which the Kellys occasionally erupt; the tentative
affairs which both have; the repeated unsuccessful attempts to
start over; and the Lake Geneva of the ending—"the dreary one
of sanatoriums and rest homes."

The unexplainable decline of the Kellys is set forth with
just the right air of vague, meaningless terror. In great part,
the effect comes from the background scenes: the beginning, in
Africa with the air black with locusts; the ending, against the
Alps in Switzerland, "a country where very few things begin, but
many things end." The reason for the Kellys' decline is made
even less explicit than Dick Diver's decline in the novel. Their
movement away from "the music and the far away lights," like
the Fitzgeralds' loss of youth and joy, ends in a question neither
can answer: "Why did we lose peace and love and health, one
after the other?" Perhaps at the heart of it is the moral answer
Fitzgerald casually introduces into the story: "There is some
wise advice in the catechism about avoiding the occasions of
sin." With its posing of an essentially moral question, its fine
shadings, and its deliberate balancing of characters, the story
is strongly reminiscent of Henry James. Among its other virtues,
the story serves to remind the reader how much continuity
Fitzgerald's writing has with the past.

Though Hollywood furnished all or part of the material for
four stories, only two found their way into collections. The
first, "Magnetism," derived from Fitzgerald's six weeks' experience
in 1927. A carefully plotted story, it makes use of Fitzgerald's
general experiences rather than specific personal ones. The
hero possesses what Fitzgerald claimed was the "top thing" and
what he himself did not have: great animal magnetism. George
Hannaford, a highly successful though limited Hollywood star,
has gained his eminence by being magnetic to those who attend
the movies as well as to the women he actually meets. The
running quarrel between him and his wife Kay, provoked by
her jealousy and her own flirtations, is much of the story. The
events include the attempted suicide of a script girl who has
been in love with George. In the final scene, his animality is
still drawing women to him, and he, unable to understand or deal
with his mysterious power, prepares to go barracuda fishing.

A more celebrated story of Hollywood is "Crazy Sunday,"

which transcribes an actual experience during Fitzgerald's second
stay there in the late months of 1931. The story is a revealing
one in its central idea—the man who makes a fool of himself
before people who count. Dwight Taylor, in his recent book, *Joy
Ride*, tells the story which Fitzgerald turned into fiction.[3] He
and Fitzgerald were invited to a party given by Irving Thalberg
and Norma Shearer. Thalberg later became the model for Monroe
Stahr in *The Last Tycoon*. The only two writers invited, both
were determined to keep Fitzgerald sober and not damage his
already fragile reputation. Fitzgerald got drunk, insulted Robert
Montgomery, and then insisted on singing a song—"a kind of
song," Taylor writes, "which might have seemed amusing if one
were very drunk and still in one's freshman year at college." No
one laughed; indeed, Jack Gilbert and Lupe Velez, "the most
liberal members of the herd," hissed. Later, while Fitzgerald was
castigating himself for the fiasco, Norma Shearer sent him a
telegram: "Dear Scott: I think you were the nicest person at my
party." He was fired, Taylor says, the next Saturday.

The story reproduces these events with great fidelity. The
song is changed to a take-off on a Jewish producer, the embarrassed writer sends a note of apology, and he receives a telegram
in return like the one cited. This central incident is expanded
into a longer story by creating a brief love affair between the
writer and the producer's wife which plays itself out after the
party. Dwight Taylor was understandably vexed to find that
Joel Coles, the drunken writer, bears Taylor's parentage (he was
the son of actress Laurette Taylor), and by such a transference,
Taylor became the man who made a fool of himself and Fitzgerald the writer who tried to save him. But the fictional background for Joel Coles does not disguise the fact that his emotional
reactions are precisely those of Fitzgerald. So is the mixture
of opportunism, conscience, guilt, and moralizing which are central to Coles's character. No perceptive reader of Fitzgerald's
fiction is likely to mistake him for anyone else.[4]

The most ambitious story—besides the Basil and Josephine
stories—to explore Fitzgerald's distant past is "The Last of the
Belles." The scene is Tarleton, Georgia, once again. The material
is out of Fitzgerald's life as a young second lieutenant at Camp
Sheridan and after. The attention is focused on "belle" Ailie
Calhoun and the three men—the narrator, Bill Knowles, and
Earl Schoen—who pursue her. The events which have counter-
parts in fact are the aviator who is killed during his courtship of

Ailie, the outfit's being sent for embarkation but not getting
past the port, and the narrator's unsuccessful courtship during
this period. Of most interest is the character Earl Schoen, a
crude, aggressive chap who looks like a streetcar conductor and
in fact was one before getting into the army. Again, the Fitzgerald belief in daring or bravado—or perhaps simply a display
of will—almost enables Earl Schoen to win Ailie Calhoun despite
his natural and cultural shortcomings that Fitzgerald somewhat
painfully emphasizes. He doesn't win her, but neither does Bill
Knowles or the narrator. The story ends six years after the war
when the narrator decides to take a trip back to Tarleton. Ailie
is going to be married to a man from Savannah. The site of the
army camp is hardly visible. "In another month," he says, "Ailie
would be gone, and the South would be empty for me forever."

Two stories that I have called uncharacteristic of Fitzgerald's
short fiction are "Family in the Wind" and "A Short Trip Home."
In the first, Fitzgerald uses a series of 1932 tornadoes in Alabama
to create background for a story whose value, to quote Arthur
Mizener, "is a result of his attempt to adjust to the wreckage of
his own career and his present condition."[5] Aside from its bearing upon his personal plight (the central character is a skilled
surgeon ruined by drink), the story shows Fitzgerald's ability
to use people, settings, and even events somewhat distant from
him in a convincing, significant way. The description of the
country people, the dialogue between members of the Janney
family, and the two tornadoes striking the town and countryside
are all done well. The story is surprisingly good in capturing the
feeling of the depression of the 1930's—a subject common enough
in the writing of the time but not so in Fitzgerald's work.

Unfortunately, the story ends in a wash of sentimentality. A
little girl is left an orphan by the storm, and Dr. Janney appears
to draw a lesson from her experience. "Daddy stood over me,"
she tells the doctor, "and I stood over kitty." He starts for
Montgomery at the end of the story, intending to resume practice. We cannot be quite sure he will succeed; he is still drawing courage from the bottle on his hip as he starts off, but he
vows to put it aside in order to assume responsibility for the
little orphan girl.

"A Short Trip Home" is better fiction, if only because it
creates such a fine sense of mystery and such a curious aura of
evil. Though Fitzgerald was obviously fond of fantasy and though
he mixes realism and fantasy in other works, this story is a most

perplexing mixture. That same comfortable world of Fitzgerald's earlier fiction is in this story inexplicably charged with evil. The evil is embodied in a creature—an incubus, perhaps—who fixes upon Ellen Baker, the eighteen-year-old Fitzgerald girl full of "that sure, clear confidence that at about eighteen begins to deepen and sing in attractive American girls." The creature's physical form is that of "a hard thin-faced man of about thirty-five."

> His eyes were a sort of taunt to the whole human family—they were the eyes of an animal, sleepy and quiescent in the presence of another species. They were helpless yet brutal, unhopeful yet confident. It was as if they felt themselves powerless to originate activity, but infinitely capable of profiting by a single gesture of weakness in another.

In the first part of the story, the man is the kind who "hangs around," who hits with brass knuckles, who engages in any shady practice the world offers him. He is, in short, a very real sinister man whom Ellen has met on the train. In the second part, he has become a "thing," a presence lurking outside the door of Ellen's compartment on the train taking them to the East. When he confronts the narrator, he is both human and fantastic—a punk who threatens the narrator with a gun but also a presence who was "getting around my abhorrence." A long struggle ensues between the narrator and "the thing"; the prize is the girl in the compartment. At its conclusion, the narrator wins, for the man is dead. "A small round hole like a larger picture nail leaves when it's pulled from a plaster wall" is in his forehead. In a few seconds, he falls to the floor. "There was something extended on the bench also—something too faint for a man, too heavy for a shadow. Even as I perceived it, it faded off and away." Ellen, inside the compartment, now sleeps peacefully; "what had possessed her had gone out of her."

The third part of the story follows the narrator's attempt to find out something about the man. An informant says his name was Joe Varland; he worked the trains; he lived off girls traveling alone. He was shot, so the man says, in a row in a station in Pittsburgh. Ellen and the narrator meet again before the story closes, but they never mention the incident.

The story is confused, but whether deliberately or carelessly is hard to say. We have to assume that Joe Varland is a corporeal being in the first part of the story; he is given explicit existence in the third part; and he is both that and a projection of the narrator's imagination in the second. But that alone does not answer for the malevolence of the man, for his sinking as the train approaches Pittsburgh, for the bullet hole in his forehead, and for his physical disappearance after he dies. This leaves a rather large burden to be carried by a genuine psychic experience on the part of the narrator which is not only general and pervasive but particular and accurate as to detail. Not much more can be done to explain the central peculiarity, but some conjectures may be made about why the story takes this form.

The story was written during those years of re-exploring the past, of thinking again about both Ginevra King and Zelda Sayre. Thus the pull is strong to explain the duality Fitzgerald saw in both women and which, fairly or not, he saw rather steadily as bountiful innocence joined with almost malignant knowingness. His own duality accented what he saw in them. Beyond that, and in all the girls he portrays, beauty is somehow entwined with evil. For at the center of Ellen's beauty lurks an evil, a corruption which threatens her self as well as those around her. Finally, Zelda's increasing obsessions help to explain the intensity with which Fitzgerald wrote this story of a woman literally possessed.

The narrator's role is one of trying to protect the girl, but of being unable to enlist her feelings or to gain her concurrence in his attempt to save her. He is not really the lover but the almost-lover, a familiar role for a Fitzgerald narrator to play. Above all other fears when in the presence of Joe Varland is the narrator's fear of being an agent, if not an accomplice. "Suddenly I realized that from a while back I had stopped hating him, stopped feeling violently alien to him. . . ." The fear aroused at this point is that of weakening or loss of will—one certainly uppermost of Fitzgerald's anxieties during the period he was writing this story. Beneath the story's climactic struggle is the silent one waged inside both Scott and Zelda when her obsession aroused his "New England conscience raised in Minnesota" to look at his own self in which will had been persistently draining away. Ultimately, the story may rest on Fitzgerald's intensely moral view in which evil is active and dominant over a will which is weak or passive. Whatever the weaknesses in the story because of its uneasy mixture of realism and fantasy, it cuts deep into the inner battle that Fitzgerald was waging then and throughout the rest of his life.

The inner conflicts and the outward circumstances of Fitzgerald's personal decline in the 1920's are matched with the decline of the Jazz Age itself in "Babylon Revisited"; in fact, it may become a period piece, so closely is it tied to that time. The story is of Charlie Wales, thirty-three, handsome, Irish, who has lived a Babylonian life during the 1920's, has reformed, and has returned to Paris to visit his daughter Honoria. The conflict is between Wales and his past; specifically it is between Wales and Marion Peters, a tight-lipped, mean-spirited woman, almost the only one of that type in Fitzgerald's fiction. Marion is the sister of Wale's deceased wife Helen, whose death is connected with a boozy quarrel in which Wales locked her out of the house in the snow. Though she recovered from pneumonia at that time and died later of heart trouble, Wales's guilt remains and Marion is unwilling to give him custody of his child.

The story is a celebrated one, with a famous line, "the snow of twenty-nine wasn't real snow. If you didn't want it to be snow, you just paid some money." It creates a nice contrast between Marion and her husband—"they were not dull people, but they were very much in the grip of life and circumstances"—and the freer spirit of Charles Wales. It is notable too for its creation of the great love and longing which exists between Wales and his daughter: "He wanted his child, and nothing was much good now, beside that fact. He wasn't young any more, with a lot of nice thoughts and dreams to have by himself. He was absolutely sure Helen wouldn't have wanted him to be so alone."

It is fitting to close this discussion of Fitzgerald's fiction during a troubled period with mention of the small number of stories which extended his range into the world of his daughter. "Outside the Cabinet-Maker's" is a delicate story of 1928, in which a couple like the Fitzgeralds buy a doll house for a six-year-old daughter (Scotty's age at the time). The father and daughter wait in the car while the mother goes into the cabinet-maker's. The parents have discussed the transaction in French to keep the secret from the girl. That small bit of "stage business" adds to the subtle central theme of the story: the impossibility, despite an intensity of love, of really entering into another loved one's world. The fantasy the father creates with the little girl as they wait, an improvised story of princesses and ogres and kings and queens, is a makeshift. Nor can his " 'Listen,' said the man to the little girl, 'I love you' " create a reality superior to the fantasy. The playful yet intense conversation never quite brings together the deepest feelings of father and daughter; momentary diversions distract each away into his separate world and keep them forever apart, however close they may be at the next moment. This is Fitzgerald's romantic vision at its most simple, most poignant: realization always falls short of the ideal; ecstatic moments never stop time; intensity of feeling never gathers the feeling itself into one clear, eternal possession.

At the very end of the period under discussion, Fitzgerald wrote a number of stories around a young girl named Gwen, obviously using his daughter—then just entering her teens—as the model for the central character. "Too Cute for Words" was published in the *Post* (April 18, 1936) and "Inside the House" (June 13, 1936). Two others were sold but not published. Though the stories are contrived in the manner of popular magazine fiction, they have some distinction as attempts to clarify family relationships about which Fitzgerald felt intensely. On the surface, the stories make the most of the conventional bewilderment of a father facing the peculiar language, desires, and fads of a young daughter.

The first story depends almost entirely on plot: Gwen's successful yet innocent attempt to escape her father's careful supervision. The second depends less on plot and more on defining the character of both father and daughter.

> It's seldom you find beauty and intelligence in the same person —a friend of the father's tells Gwen—When you do they have to spend the first part of their life terribly afraid of a flame they'll have to put out someday—and sometime they spend the rest of their life trying to wake up that same flame . . . one of the sticks is the beauty they have lost and the other is the intelligence they haven't cultivated—and the two sticks won't make a bonfire.

The lesson is, of course, Fitzgerald's own; and this note of rather pathetic analysis runs through Fitzgerald's writing during the mid-1930's, his time of deepest despair.

CHAPTER 8

Tender Is the Night

S HORTLY AFTER her second breakdown in 1932, Zelda Fitzgerald began writing an autobiographical novel. She sub-
mitted the manuscript directly to Maxwell Perkins of Scribner's;
when Fitzgerald found out about it, he reacted somewhat as if
his worst rival had just stolen his best idea. "My God," he wrote,
"my books made her a legend and her single intention in this
somewhat thin portrait is to make me a non-entity."[1] When his
anger subsided, he worked with Perkins to get the novel published; he felt, and probably correctly, that she needed the feel
of success associated "with work done in a workmanlike manner
for its own sake." In the revised version, the attack on Fitzgerald is blunted (Amory Blaine is no longer the name of the
central male character), and the published book offers a view
of the Fitzgeralds' lives not unlike that seen in Fitzgerald's
own fiction.

Save Me the Waltz, as the novel was called, covers in a
febrile, impressionistic prose the whole span of Zelda Sayre's
life, but it focuses on the years between Fitzgerald's courtship
and the death of Judge Sayre in 1931. The central character
is Alabama Beggs; the young officer who wins her is David
Knight, not a writer but an artist. The events tally precisely
with those of real life. After the wedding, she and David are
sitting on the bed in a room in the Biltmore reading the papers.
"'We're having people,' everybody said to everybody else, 'and
we want you to join us.'" The "twilights after the war," as Zelda
called them, emerge from her prose much as they must have
appeared to the Fitzgeralds at the time. Even more of the intensity, the shifting colors, and the clamor is in the chapters describing the years 1921-24 than in Fitzgerald's stories of the period.

The central part of the story is devoted to Alabama's dancing
career, Zelda Fitzgerald's own obsession. The last part finds
the Knights back in her parents' Southern town just before her

father dies. The very last scene finds their child playing at grand-mother's house saying, "We shall be gone soon," and the other replying, "You people never stay anywhere." At the end, Alabama and David are sitting "in the pleasant gloom of late afternoon staring at each other through the remains of the party."

The book is in its way as poignant as *Tender Is the Night*, although not so deeply affecting. Though written during her recovery from her second breakdown, it has more life and vigor (but a good deal less control) than *Tender Is the Night*. It is almost as if we see reflected in the two books both the warring and complementary characteristics of the two Fitzgeralds: two kinds of brilliance unable to outdazzle the other; two innocents living "by the infinite promise of American advertising"; two restless temperaments craving both excitement and repose. Each book embodies the powerful drive of its creator which was, often as not, antagonistic to the drive of the other. "A strange thing was," Fitzgerald wrote to Laura Guthrie, "I could never convince her that I was a first-rate writer." Or, as Zelda expressed Alabama's unwillingness to yield in the novel, "David David Knight Knight Knight, for instance, couldn't possibly make her put out her light till she got good and ready."

Both *Save Me the Waltz* and *Tender Is the Night* are depressing books because only with difficulty can they be torn from the sad particulars of the Fitzgeralds' fate. If the 1920's described in both books sometimes seems like a prelude to disaster, the 1930's is disaster itself. From the time he returned permanently to America (1932) until his death, Fitzgerald was never more than momentarily free from the spectre of his wife's insanity, from his own alcoholism, and from the responsibility of keeping life going for himself, Zelda, and their daughter, now entering her teens.

"Our united front," he wrote, referring to the quiet life he was forcing them to lead in 1932, "is less a romance than a categorical imperative." And yet, the battle was only a holding action. After her second breakdown, there was a period—from the spring of 1932 to the end of 1933—when Zelda could be at La Paix. But this period was an uneasy one: "All through the year and a half we lived in the country, . . . there would be episodes of great gravity that seemed to have no 'build-up,' outbursts of temper, violence, rashness, etc. that could neither be foreseen or forestalled."[2] The best moments were those with the children which Andrew Turnbull has described so well in his recent book.[3]

When a fire destroyed the upper floor of La Paix, the house was not repaired, and they lived on in that symbolic shell until December, 1933, when they moved to a smaller house at 1307 Park Avenue, Baltimore. During this time and in the years to follow, Fitzgerald spent an increasing amount of time in the hospital, sometimes for physical illness, at others for general recuperation from prolonged drinking. His drinking led to quarrels with both Hemingway and Edmund Wilson; these, like those with Zelda, left him tormented by a kind of feeling he described in another connection: "How strange to have failed as a social creature." He continued, however, to see people. He visited T. S. Eliot when he gave the Turnbull lecture at Johns Hopkins in 1932. He became interested in communism and invited to La Paix a number of party spokesmen who ended up by boring him. He took trips, usually ending in drunkenness, to New York. He wrote a good deal, but most of the time in short bursts sustained by alcohol. His best efforts went into *Tender Is the Night*, and the small number of magazine articles and stories produced meant that his income dropped below his expenses once again. For a number of years, royalties from his previous books had dropped to less than fifty dollars. In 1929, he earned $31.77 from all his books.

At Christmas time in 1933 the Fitzgeralds went to Bermuda for a vacation. Unfortunately, Fitzgerald came down with pleurisy, Zelda was fighting off her third breakdown, and the trip must have seemed like those of the worst days in Europe. Shortly after they returned, she was forced to go back to the clinic at Johns Hopkins. Later in the year, after an attempted suicide, she was sent to another sanitarium in upstate New York. From there, she came back to Baltimore worse than before. In August, 1934, Fitzgerald wrote that he had spent an hour and a half with her and had found her much better than she had been previously that year. But such a period of hope only came with increasing periods of confinement. From 1934 until Fitzgerald's death—and for that matter until her own death—Zelda Fitzgerald was unable to maintain a normal existence in the world for long.

Through this vastly troubling period, Fitzgerald worked to bring *Tender Is the Night* into publishable form. The novel, unlike his other work, has a long history.[4] It goes back to the novel he began work on soon after the publication of *The Great Gatsby*. In August, 1925, he had written to Maxwell Perkins about a new novel "about Zelda and me and the hysteria of last June in Paris." The plot, however, was based upon "an intellectual murder on the Leopold–Loeb idea." He first called it "Our Type," but at other times it was entitled "The World's Fair," "The Melarky Case," and "The Boy Who Killed His Mother." Pieces of it got into "The Drunkard's Holiday" and "Doctor Diver's Holiday," the immediate predecessors of *Tender Is the Night*.

Malcolm Cowley, in his 1951 edition of the novel, has described the three separate versions of it. (Matthew Bruccoli, in a more recent study of the manuscripts, notes three versions and eighteen stages of composition.) In April, 1926, Fitzgerald said he had a fourth of the novel done and was planning to finish it that year. But work went badly and only four chapters of this first version are now extant. A good deal of this material was worked into the early parts of *Tender Is the Night*, but emphasis and plot and final intention were so changed as to make the original version a distant cousin to the final one.

The main differences and similarities can be seen in "The World's Fair" section of the manuscript, part four of which has been published in *The Kenyon Review* (Autumn, 1948) and in the appendix to Cowley's edition of the novel. The world's fair of this novel is seen through the eyes of young Francis Melarky, a technician from Hollywood, who is intended to be handsome and intelligent and to have the makings of a first-rate man. The novel was planned to show the forces working on Melarky to drive him into a love affair with Dinah Piper, to attempt to keep pace with the international set on the Riviera, and eventually to kill his mother in a fit of rage. The tone suggests something of a story, like *Gatsby*, with the *haute monde* making its assault on a provincial but highly developed sensibility.

How Fitzgerald worked sections of this material into *Tender Is the Night* can be illustrated by comparing portions of "The World's Fair" with the same portions worked into the novel. One such scene is the Wanda Breasted episode, reprinted both in Cowley's edition and in *The Kenyon Review*. What provoked Fitzgerald to include this scene in Chapter 17, Book One, of *Tender Is the Night* must have been the arresting way he described a trio of women, "rather like long-stemmed flowers and rather like cobra's heads," and the pieces of dialogue used to describe the Pipers (Divers): "I prefer people whose lives have more corrugated surfaces." There is also the larger purpose in both versions of the novel of letting Francis Melarky in the earliest version (Rosemary Hoyt in the published one) see the

Pipers (Divers) through the kind of subterranean talk that is malicious but partly true.

The second version of the novel was probably written in 1929 after Fitzgerald had pretty much given up the design of the Melarky novel. In this version, Rosemary Hoyt and her mother meet the Divers (now called Lewellen and Nicole Kelly) on board a ship bound for the Riviera. Rosemary's introduction to the Riviera, with which the published version of *Tender Is the Night* begins, uses much of the material from Chapter I of the Melarky story which had Francis and his mother arriving under similar circumstances. In both episodes, the innocent outsider— Francis Melarky in one, Rosemary Hoyt in the other—is used as a means of disclosing that carnival world of which the Divers seem to be the center. The two stories—Rosemary Hoyt's and Dick Diver's—which seem to fit uneasily together in *Tender Is the Night*, fail to fuse because, over the long history of the novel's creation, Fitzgerald seems unable to decide which shall be central. The most obvious vestige of the Melarky story which still remains in *Tender Is the Night* is the attention given to Rosemary's mother, an attention vital to a novel in which the child is going to murder the mother but intrusive in one in which that child is not even going to be the principal character and the mother much less than that.

In *Tender Is the Night*, the characters through which the innocent learns of a richer, larger life have become the main characters in the story. Instead of the Divers illuminating the life of Francis Melarky or Rosemary Hoyt, the latter bring us into understanding of the Divers. For this version, Fitzgerald wrote a long outline in which the story of Dick Diver is so clearly in mind that it is unnecessary to mention Rosemary in describing the plot:

> The novel should do this. Show a man who is a natural idealist, a spoiled priest, giving in for various causes to the ideas of the haute Burgeoise, and in his rise to the top of the social world, losing his idealism, his talent and turning to drink and dissipation. Background one in which the leisure class is at their truly most brilliant and glamorous such as Murphys.
>
> The hero born in 1891 is a man like myself brought up in a family sunk from haute burgeoisie to petit burgeoisie, yet expensively educated. He has all the gifts, and goes through Yale almost succeeding but not quite. . . .[5]

Most of the writing of *Tender Is the Night* from the point
of this outline on was done at La Paix in 1932 and 1933. Fitzgerald was thinking of forty-one thousand additional words in
January and was also hoping to get it done by staying sober from
February to April. Despite Zelda's second breakdown, he was
apparently well enough along by spring, 1932, to hope for
publication the following year. By early fall, he could envision
getting the first installment for serialization to Scribner's by
October. It was not until a year later, however, that the manuscript could be sent for final editing. Serialization began in the
January, 1934, issue of *Scribner's* and ran in four issues. It was
published in book form in April, 1934.

I *Criticism of Tender Is the Night*

Tender Is the Night, the hardest of Fitzgerald's books to
judge, is understandably the one about which competent critics
have expressed the widest range of opinions. Its weaknesses have
been suggested in recounting its creation. Chiefly they have to
do with the structure of the book and its characterizations.

The uneasiness Fitzgerald felt toward the structure of the
book caused him to change the order of the chapters in a re-
consideration of the novel in 1938. "Its great fault," he wrote,
"is that the true beginning—the young psychiatrist in Switzerland
—is tucked away in the middle of the book." Malcolm Cowley
has edited the novel in the order Fitzgerald's marked copy suggests. The principal change is to make Book Two, the story of
Dick Diver, the beginning of the novel and to have the Rosemary
material, with which the novel began, the second book. The
course of the novel and the conclusion remain the same.

There is no question that the novel in this revised form is
a more straightforward story. Dick Diver, an extremely promising
young psychiatrist, falls in love with Nicole, a rich mental patient,
marries her, and for various reasons declines into obscurity
while she grows capable of facing the world without him. The
affair with Rosemary Hoyt is a brief and necessary break away
from the regimen that his marriage to Nicole has imposed upon
him and dramatizes the selfless character of his devotion to his
wife. The life on the Riviera is no longer presented as "la dolce
vita," but as a life forced upon the Divers by Nicole's condition.
Such a story can hardly escape banality unless the reader feels

the intensity of Dick's love for Nicole, which causes him to sacrifice himself that she may regain her health.

To readers coming to the story directly, without being distracted by the Rosemary story, Dick Diver and Nicole may be sufficiently distinctive (and their lives sufficiently symbolic of many disordered lives) to carry the weight of seriousness expected of them. With its emphasis upon psychiatry, the novel offers a case history of a rational man being destroyed by the forces of irrationality. Even so, there is much that is merely pathetic in Dick's giving up at thirty-eight, much that is contrived in Baby Warren's using of Dick, and much that is unconvincing in the "transference" that cures Nicole initially and hands her on to Tommy Barban at the end. Worst of all, the two central characters are flat, perhaps because Fitzgerald had worked too often with them under various guises in the past to be able to present them freshly and vividly.

Part of Dick Diver's lack of substance can be blamed upon Fitzgerald's tendency to shirk the full creation of his ideal characters—to create a shimmering surface and pass it off as having genuine substance. What would do for short fiction, what staggers a bit in *The Beautiful and Damned,* cannot bear the weight assigned to it in *Tender Is the Night.* In many respects, Dick Diver in the Rosemary episodes—whether that section comes first or second—is not the Dick Diver, medical student and psychiatrist, of the rest of the book. With Rosemary he is all surface, not because he has changed from his early days at Zurich, but because he is a simulacrum cut from any of dozens of stories projecting one aspect or another of Fitzgerald's romantic hero. There is a similar disconnection between Nicole as the wife of Dr. Diver and Nicole as the psychiatric patient who has been raped by her father. Fitzgerald was trying for something very hard to achieve. He was placing a deliberately glossy surface upon the Divers' life to create a sense of both mystery and worth. He had succeeded with Gatsby partly because Gatsby's very character required that he be left shadowy. He does not succeed in *Tender Is the Night,* where the necessary specification of character turns the novel into a somewhat chic story of the analyst who falls in love with his patient and the troubles to which that leads.

Whether the published edition or Fitzgerald's revised version is the better structure is a moot point. Neither one nor the other endows the central characters with magnitude or makes the central situation other than pathetic. Though the novel gains in directness and focus by placing the Diver story first, it loses much of the atmosphere and mystery brilliantly created in the Rosemary section. In both versions, the evidence of material written at different times in different moods and at different levels of inspiration is too often apparent.

There is simply too much hinted at, too little fulfilled. A novel about moral innocence coming into worldly awareness seems never to have completely left Fitzgerald's mind. It appears openly in the Rosemary section; it is often at the edge of Dick Diver's relationship with the Warrens and with Abe North; it appears in a comic way in the character of McKisco. Another novel, one like Thackeray's *Vanity Fair* but drawing seriously upon the confrontation of capitalism and communism, also runs through the material. The young man ruined by money, the young girl debauched by money, and the world debased by money are hinted at repeatedly. In the opposition of Dick Diver, the clergyman's son, to the Warrens, the Chicago exploiters, Fitzgerald has the makings of a novel which would use its characters to dramatize a larger conflict within American society. Still another novel is the introspective one which seems to assert its power when Fitzgerald becomes most intensely involved in the relationship between Dick and Nicole. Suggesting these possibilities helps explain why many critics regard *Tender Is the Night* as the richest of Fitzgerald's novels.

The reviews of *Tender Is the Night* were more favorable than unfavorable,[6] but the book did not do well, either in restoring a measure of Fitzgerald's reputation or at the bookstores. It sold thirteen thousand copies, the least of any of Fitzgerald's novels.

II *After Tender Is the Night*

Disappointing as the reviews and the sales were, they were not unexpected. Fitzgerald's fees as a magazine writer had been dropping because of the Depression and because he was going somewhat out of fashion. The struggle to get a novel written had apparently not been so much one to reach the highest goals as to get the task done in a respectable fashion. "If I had one more crack at it cold sober," he wrote, "I believe it might have made a great difference."

But Fitzgerald was too much of a professional to be crushed by any response other than complete rejection. He began work almost immediately on a historical novel about medieval life, *The Count of Darkness,* published in four installments in *Red Book* in 1934, 1935, and 1941. He also finished three stories and two articles and completed the compiling and proofing of *Taps at Reveille,* for publication in March, 1935.

Most of the stories in *Taps at Reveille* have already been discussed—the Basil Duke Lee stories in Chapter I, the others in Chapter VII. The volume is the largest of Fitzgerald's collections and selects from a much larger group of stories. It is an important collection because it is the only one published in his lifetime which reveals his range. Of all Fitzgerald's books, however, *Taps at Reveille* received the least attention and sold most poorly. It deserved better, but a review by William Troy in *The Nation* was almost the only one to see its merits. Even that review said less about the stories than about Fitzgerald as a writer, and it ended by sententiously calling Fitzgerald's "moral vision" vague and immature. Troy was, however, sensitive to the quality of Fitzgerald's short fiction which still gives it distinction:

> The problem of character, which is first and last the moral problem, is not popular with many writers of current fiction. . . . What used to be called character has dissolved in the confused welter of uncoordinated actions, sensations, impressions, and physico-chemical reactions which currently passes for the art of fiction.
>
> Mr. Fitzgerald, in his persistent concentration on "those fine moral decisions that people make in books" is fundamentally, therefore, an old-fashioned sort of story-teller. He has more in common, let us say, with George Eliot, Henry James, and Joseph Conrad than with any of the more prominent members of his own generation.[7]

Debt, cirrhosis of the liver, the fight to stay sober, and an attack of tuberculosis forced Fitzgerald closer to the wall in 1935 than he had ever been. He wrote of his crack-up in a dispassionate, precise style as brilliant as had appeared in any of his previous fiction. But from 1935 on, his fiction took a turn away from his earlier work, though at the very last he was working on *The Last Tycoon* as a novel which would make full use of what he had learned in writing both *The Great Gatsby* and *Tender Is the Night.*

CHAPTER 9

The Crack-Up *and After*

THREE ESSAYS—"The Crack-Up," "Pasting It Together," and "Handle with Care," which appeared in *Esquire* in February, March, and April, 1935—have done much to sustain Fitzgerald's reputation even as they described his actual decline. Though such undisguised self-revelation displeased his literary friends, the essays are of a piece with the self-dramatization that was Fitzgerald's strength. Whether they are precisely true, whether they conceal or mask the real condition, is beside the point. Like his best fiction, the essays have a truth to the character created in them. The delicate handling of the narrator as both observer and observed, the movement from awareness to a precise kind of bitterness, and the elegance of the prose are aesthetic values of a high order. Although presented as autobiography, they have the air of highly wrought and intensely felt fiction. They are justifiably famous; taken together, they constitute one of the superb short stories in American literature.

These essays are part of a good deal of writing Fitzgerald was able to do even when he was near the bottom of his physical and emotional resources. In 1936, he published eleven stories and sketches in the *Post*, the *American Magazine*, *McCall's*, and *Esquire*. From this point on, there was a sharp decline in the amount of writing and some falling off in quality, though Fitzgerald was not grossly exaggerating when he said he was incapable of writing anything really bad. The years 1938 and 1939 are clearly his leanest, for "Financing Finnegan" was the only published story to appear between January, 1938, and November, 1939. Then, as if the writer he described in the last "Crack-Up" essay had really emerged, another flurry of work produced six stories, the seventeen stories in the Pat Hobby series, and *The Last Tycoon*, written in the last two years of his life.

The material of these last five years can be related to three moods reflected in the "Crack-Up" essays. In the first essay, Fitzgerald describes his crack-up and contrasts his present self with various images of the "successful" writer he once was. In the second, he focuses on specific early disappointments which foreshadowed his later disintegration. In the third, he resolves to abandon any attempt to be a "sentient adult" and to become a writer only.

The first of these moods discloses itself in the autobiographical pieces: "Early Success" (1937), and those published in *Esquire* in 1936—"An Author's Mother," "Author's House," and "Afternoon of an Author." Not quite fiction but not clearly autobiography, they gain strength from the direct and implied contrasts between the greatly successful author of the 1920's and the man in the mirror ten years later: "The perfect neurotic. By-product of an idea, slag of a dream." How well Fitzgerald can capture his two selves and the feeling toward the one as toward the other, is displayed at the conclusion of "Author's House." The author takes his guest up to the cupola—"the turret, the watchtower, whatever you want to call it."

> It is small up there and full of baked silent heat until the author opens two of the glass sides that surround it and the twilight wind blows through. As far as your eye can see there is a river winding between green lawns and trees and purple buildings and red slums blended in by a merciful dusk. Even as they stand there the wind increases until it is a gale whistling around the tower and blowing birds past them.
> "I lived up here once," the author said after a moment.
> "Here? For a long time?"
> "No. For just a little while when I was young."
> "It must have been rather cramped."
> "I didn't notice it."
> "Would you like to try it again?"
> "No. And I couldn't if I wanted to."[1]

The second of these moods appears briefly in a number of stories and sketches of the mid-1930's. Two *Esquire* stories published later in 1936, "I Didn't Get Over" and "Send Me in, Coach," promise to be explicit accounts of two such failures, but choose to treat the announced subjects by implication only. Thus, the first is not so much about Fitzgerald's disappointment in not getting overseas during the war as it is about the snubs he suffered or thought he suffered all his life. Similarly, the second does not concern the young Fitzgerald yearning to prove himself on the football field; the scene is a boy's camp and the action is restricted to the rehearsal of a play in which the principal line is "So, coach, you think we cannot win without Playfair." The impact of the story comes from the news which arrives during the rehearsal that the father of one of the boys has just shot himself.

The final mood is clearly evident in the large number of sketches and stories which seem cut off from Fitzgerald's feelings but which still disclose his craft as a writer. The Pat Hobby stories comprise the largest number of these. Beginning in *Esquire* in January, 1940, with "Pat Hobby's Christmas Wish," seventeen such stories—one a month—were published. These stories are remarkable for their almost complete detachment from feeling and, therefore, from the affective impulse of most of Fitzgerald's previous fiction. We do not sympathize with or condemn Pat Hobby, and we are not expected to. Nor, despite the continuing satire of Hollywood people and manners, are we aroused to feel strongly about either the people or the place. The attention is concentrated on the craft with which Fitzgerald manipulates his stuffed men and woman on his puppet stage as he runs Pat Hobby, the has-been Hollywood script writer, through a variety of temporary successes, deceptions, and ultimate defeats.

In one story, Pat repays an actor's snub by disclosing that the terrifyingly real war scene which made him famous gained its power because the actor was scared stiff when the episode was filmed on the studio lot. In another, Pat is revealed for the drunkard he is by someone's bringing in a sack of empty bottles Pat has been trying to dispose of secretly. In another, he arranges to take a girl to a preview of "his" movie. Though at first he is barred from the theatre, he gets in when the playwright who worked with him on the script walks out, leaving full credit to Pat. The picture is so bad that the playwright refuses to have anything to do with it. All the stories turn on the attempts of Pat Hobby to work his way into some kind of writing job. The clumsiness of his deceptions and his real innocence despite his imagined shrewdness betray him more often than not. Nevertheless, he never really becomes bitter nor do the powers in Hollywood ever quite lose their affection for him. The recent complete collection of Pat Hobby stories (Scribner's, 1962) is likely to bring too many of them before the reader at one time. Read singly, the stories leave the impression of minor but distinctive achievements.

Since the majority of the stories of these years draw heavily upon Fitzgerald's present or past experiences, most of the details of his life between 1935 and 1940 can be found in one story or another. The broken collarbone he suffered in a diving accident in July, 1936 (he was showing off for a nurse), appears in an *Esquire* story, "Design in Plaster," written in July, 1938. "Financing Finnegan" treats directly and ironically the difficulties he presented for his literary agent, Harold Ober. "Trouble" (*Post*, 1937) is a hospital story, a typical Fitzgerald romance between a trained nurse nicknamed "Trouble" and a proper young doctor. "An Alcoholic Case" (*Esquire*, 1937) describes, from the nurse's point of view, the difficulties of taking care of an alcoholic cartoonist. "The Lost Decade" (*Esquire*, 1939) is a short sketch about an alcoholic who has literally lost ten years. "The Long Way Out," reprinted in the recent Scribner's collection, is a brief, terrifying account of a woman who, like Zelda, is confined to a sanitarium. The hat which figures so prominently in that story is like one she was wearing in 1936, when, as Arthur Mizener described it, "the friend found her at the station, exquisitely dressed, a thoroughly sophisticated woman, except that she was wearing a hat like a child's bonnet with the strings carefully knotted under her chin."[2]

In structure, the stories of these last years fall into two groups: the very short, sketch-like stories, and the long stories which attempt to control a large body of material. The turn to the sketch and the weaknesses in the longer stories point to a major decline in Fitzgerald's ability to control the many events with which his long stories often swarm. "Too much about all sorts of major and minor irrelevancies," one magazine editor wrote in rejecting a long story. Fitzgerald's last three long stories are "The End of Hate," "Discard," and "The Last Kiss." "The End of Hate," rejected several times before *Collier's* printed it in 1940, is a romantic Civil War story in which Rebel boy eventually wins Union girl. The germ of the story probably came from stories of the War told to Fitzgerald by his father. The other two, both published after his death (*Harper's Bazaar*, January, 1948; *Collier's*, April 16, 1949), are about Hollywood.

There are few good stories from these last years. The worst are plot stories like "Strange Sanctuary" (*Liberty*, 1939), "The Intimate Strangers" (*McCall's*, 1935), or "In the Holidays" (*Esquire*, 1937). Aside from the autobiographical pieces, only four stories from mid-1935 to 1941 have been put into collections.

Of these, the best single story is probably "Three Hours Between Planes" (*Esquire*, 1941), which makes the most of a small but pleasing idea, a comic variation on the theme of a man trying to regain a part of his past. The most intensely felt and the most brilliant writing is to be found in the autobiographical pieces, some of which may be regarded as fiction: "Author's House," "Afternoon of an Author," and "The Crack-Up" essays themselves.

I *Fitzgerald's Last Years*

Fitzgerald's life from 1935 on is one of continuing physical deterioration. Zelda's illness of the past five years had exhausted hope of her recovery. Now he had to face his own physical ills. The visit to the doctor described in "The Crack-Up" confronted him with evidence of active tuberculosis. His response was the retreat he so carefully described in that essay. The actual withdrawal was to Henderson, North Carolina, where he stayed a month, living very cheaply, as he wrote in his Ledger: "Today I am in comparative affluence, but Monday and Tuesday I had two tins of potted meat, three oranges and a box of Uneedas and two cans of beer."[3] He washed out his one shirt and two handkerchiefs in the washbowl at night. Debt hung over him. He wrote of being "not only thousands, nay tens of thousands in debt . . . less than forty cents cash in the world and probably a deficit at my bank."

At Christmas time, 1935, he returned to Baltimore where he had been maintaining an apartment across from the Johns Hopkins campus. In April of the next year, Zelda Fitzgerald was placed in Highland Sanitarium near Asheville, North Carolina. Though she was able to visit outside the sanitarium and spent a considerable period with her mother in Montgomery, Alabama, after Fitzgerald's death, Highland was her permanent home until her death in the fire which destroyed the sanitarium in 1948. For most of 1936 and 1937, Fitzgerald lived in Asheville, trying to provide Zelda some respite from her confinement. He was still drinking heavily, still feeling a sense of disintegration; twice he tried to commit suicide.

In September, 1936, his mother died leaving him $42,000, a small part of which he already owed to the estate. Letters written to friends during this period reflect moods swinging between not giving a "good Goddam" and feeling freed for "other mischief such as work." By June, 1937, he had made arrangements to go to M-G-M for six months at $1,000 a week. "The Garden of Allah," Hollywood, became his temporary address.

Hollywood was probably more endurable for Fitzgerald at the end of his career than it had been earlier. Despite the fact that his work, early and late, attracted the attention of producers and directors, Fitzgerald never turned to Hollywood except for a quick assignment or, at the end, in desperation. His two earlier script assignments had been competently completed on his part, but neither picture was produced. Frustration of one kind or another marked his periods of Hollywood employment.

The Pat Hobby stories and even *The Last Tycoon* show a certain acceptance of Hollywood; Fitzgerald knows more about it but seems to care less. Almost all of the earlier stories about Hollywood are mildly or sharply satirical. "Zone of Accident" (*Post*, 1935) begins with the appearance of a Hollywood star in the emergency room of a Baltimore hospital, her back slashed from waist to shoulder. A central scene is a beauty contest seeking talent for Hollywood, which Fitzgerald describes in a sustained mood of great contempt. Though the story ends by bringing the young interne and the Hollywood star together, her decision to leave Hollywood, if she can find anything better, is probably not far from Fitzgerald's attitude over the years. The difficulty in 1937 was that there did not seem to be anything as good.

He worked on a good many scripts: *Three Comrades, A Yank at Oxford, Infidelity, The Women, Madame Curie,* and *Gone with the Wind,* but such work was piecemeal and frustrating to a writer who for so long had had complete responsibility for his work. The Pat Hobby stories and *The Last Tycoon* are the most important writings outside the work done for the movies. To the public, his sad trip to Dartmouth early in 1939 to make *Winter Carnival* and his love affair with Sheilah Graham are the notable events of these years. Each furnished the material for a best-selling book after Fitzgerald's death: *The Disenchanted,* by Budd Schulberg, and *Beloved Infidel* by Sheilah Graham and Gerold Frank. Neither book was worthy of its subject. To these aspects of his personal life should be added the relationship with his daughter; always a close one, it became even closer when Scotty became a Vassar student and interested in writing. The letters to her, in part collected in *The Crack-Up,* are not so much personal as literary ones—a putting of himself on record for himself, Scotty, and posterity.

The relationship between Fitzgerald and his daughter, as between Fitzgerald and Sheilah Graham, brings out an important aspect of Fitzgerald's character. His legendary self conceals the fact that he was a born teacher, a would-be scholar. "The fine quiet of the scholar," he wrote in *Tender Is the Night*, "which is nearest of all things to heavenly peace." We conjecture that his attraction to Sheilah Graham was in part the challenge of educating her. The reading lists he compiled for her, the books he provided, are a curious part of that romance. Similarly, the letters to Scotty are Fitzgerald's kind of pedantry brilliantly expressed:

> Poetry is either something that lives like fire inside you—like music to the musician or Marxism to the Communist—or else it is nothing, an empty, formalized bore, around which pedants can endlessly drone their notes and explanations. *The Grecian Urn* is unbearably beautiful, with every syllable as inevitable as the notes in Beethoven's Ninth Symphony, or it's just something you don't understand. It is what it is because an extraordinary genius paused at that point in history and touched it. I suppose I've read it a hundred times. About the tenth time I began to know what it was about, and caught the chime in it and the exquisite inner mechanics. . . . For awhile after you quit Keats all other poetry seems to be only whistling or humming.[4]

Through his first long stint in Hollywood—from June, 1937, to January, 1939—Fitzgerald was paying a fixed amount of his income toward retirement of a debt estimated at $40,000 in 1937. The period spent in Doctor's Hospital, New York, recounted by Schulberg in *The Disenchanted*, was followed by a longer one upon his returning to New York from a vacation in Cuba with Zelda in 1939. He broke off his long relationship with Harold Ober in summer partly as a result of a quarrel about an advance but also because of general difficulty in maintaining close personal relationships. By the end of September, 1939, he began to work on a novel, *The Last Tycoon*, which he left unfinished at his death. *Collier's* was talking of paying $25,000 or $30,000 for the serial rights, but neither *Collier's* nor the *Post* would commit themselves on the basis of the six thousand words he was able to show at that time. With debts pressing upon him and with no movie contract through 1939 and early 1940, he took time to write "The Last Kiss," his last story. In April, 1940, he had a chance to work on the script of "Babylon Revisited," which he had sold to the movies not long before. The movie was never produced, nor has the script, "The Cosmopolitan," been published, although it is a very interesting revision of the original story.

A measure of Fitzgerald's difficulties in writing for the movies is disclosed in this note which prefaced "The Cosmopolitan" script: "This is an attempt to tell a story from a child's point of view without sentimentality. Any attempt to heighten the sentiment of the early scenes by putting mawkish speeches into the mouth of characters—in short by doing what is locally known as 'milking it,' will damage the *force* of the piece. . . . So whoever deals with this script is implored to remember that it is *a dramatic piece*—not a homey family story. Above all things, Victoria is a *child*—not Daddy's little helper who knows all the answers."

II *The Last Tycoon*

The Last Tycoon, the novel Fitzgerald left unfinished at his death, was edited by Edmund Wilson and published by Scribner's the year after his death. It is an extensive fragment of about sixty thousand words shaped into six consecutive chapters and with extensive notes, outlines, and partially written sections filling out the design. Its publication was accompanied by a good many reviews hinting that only its incompleteness prevented it from being Fitzgerald's masterpiece.

As early as 1945, however, more judicious considerations of Fitzgerald's work modified such praise. In one critic's words, "its promise has been extravagantly overestimated for the most generous reasons by his friends."[5] The *Times Literary Supplement* admitted that the novel had "a kind of distinction that clung to Fitzgerald's writing," but its reviewer concluded that the "final version of *The Last Tycoon* would have been readable but thoroughly second-rate."[6] It is hard not to agree with the *Times* verdict. Perhaps the most that can be said is that Fitzgerald would probably have improved upon the completed chapters of the novel and enhanced the rather barren outline in finishing it.

The novel is, in some ways, a departure from Fitzgerald's previous work. It is set on a larger stage, and brings into the story a world affected by politics, labor strife, and ideology. Its examination of an industry—Hollywood's movie industry—promises to be more accurate and complete than that given to psychiatry in *Tender Is the Night* or to Long Island life of the 1920's in *The Great Gatsby*. The plot leans more heavily upon the intrigues, the economic struggles, and the contests for power than upon the personal struggles of a central character. The larger political issues which almost got into *Tender Is the Night* enter *The Last Tycoon* with the appearance of Brimmer, a member of the Communist party, who represents the militant demands of the union against the benevolent paternalism of Monroe Stahr.

In its intentions, at least, it may have been the most conscientious and informed novel to be written about Hollywood. But even that intent raises the question of whether a great novel is likely to result from a documentary study, and particularly from one of such a limited and artificial world as Hollywood. Despite all the care Fitzgerald took to make *The Last Tycoon* authentic, the novel seldom communicates the sense and feel of Hollywood in the way that such a partial, impressionistic novel as Nathanael West's *Day of the Locust* does.

In other respects, the novel can be compared with both *The Great Gatsby* and *Tender Is the Night*. The choice of narrator, Cecilia Brady, is a return to the technique used in *The Great Gatsby*, but the character is imperfectly realized and simply shoved off the scene when it suits the author. There seems little evidence that, given her character and the situation in the novel, she could have given to the novel the unity of tone, the point of view, and the reflective moral center which so tightly creates *The Great Gatsby*.

The melodrama, which the general excellence of *The Great Gatsby* tends to minimize, seems destined to be an obvious and more important part of *The Last Tycoon*. What may be called Fitzgerald's "murderous fancies" make the whole last half of the novel revolve around Stahr's hiring of an assassin to kill his partner, Brady. It would have been difficult to bring off such extreme action in relation to the rest of the story—more difficult even than glossing over the contrivance in the accidental death of Myrtle Wilson.

Finally, the love story of *The Last Tycoon* is the Gatsby story once again. Here it is Stahr's memory of his deceased wife, Minna, that draws him to Kathleen. Unfortunately, Kathleen is visible, detailed, and specific; hers is not the shadowy reality given to Daisy. Considering that she must make the high passion of Stahr credible, she is, as created in the completed part of the novel, fatally inadequate. "Where will the warmth come from," Fitzgerald wrote in his notes. "My girls were all so warm and full of promise. What can I do to make it honest and different?"

The resemblances of *The Last Tycoon* to *Tender Is the Night* are to be found in the explicitness of detail. Though Fitzgerald imagined the finished novel as having about sixty thousand words, he had written seventy thousand words into less than the first half. As in *Tender Is the Night,* the canvas is larger, the cast of characters larger, and the purposes multiple rather than single. Though rewriting would undoubtedly have tightened it, it could hardly have resulted in the compactness of *The Great Gatsby.* Fitzgerald's writing seems to have undergone an irreversible change toward inclusion, specification, and elaboration; it was as if he no longer could rely on the magical evocative power of style that made *The Great Gatsby* do so much in so few words. The structure of *The Last Tycoon,* like that of *Tender Is the Night,* tends toward the creation of two insufficiently related stories, Stahr's love and Stahr's struggles in Hollywood. Finally, Monroe Stahr, like Dick Diver, suffers as a fictional character from being constantly urged into a greatness which the details of his past and his present actions fail to support. Since the author urges so much, the reader can hardly fail to be disappointed when the character succeeds in being only fitfully pathetic, never tragic, and at times something of a bore.

Of *The Last Tycoon,* we are forced to admit as true what Fitzgerald said of it: "It is an escape into a lavish, romantic past that perhaps will not come again in our time." It is curious that this admission came at the end of a long summary of the story in which he claimed it would be more like *The Great Gatsby* than *Tender Is the Night.* He seems to have passed over the fact that *Gatsby* is not an escape into a romantic past, but an intense examination of the attractiveness and yet the impossibility of that escape. What Fitzgerald proposes in *The Last Tycoon* is to give substance to the visions of *The Great Gatsby* and to try to make them solid, true, and interesting.

It is too much to ask that F. Scott Fitzgerald cap the successes of his youth and compensate for the failure of his last years with his greatest work. It would be too much like a second-rate Fitzgerald story. Yet, it is entirely right that Fitzgerald was working so hard and so seriously at his craft when he died. There is more than mere vanity in his letter to his daughter six months before his death: "I am not a great man but sometimes I think the impersonal and objective quality of my talent and the sacrifices of it, in pieces, to preserve its essential value has some sort of epic grandeur." All the pathos of his career is found in another letter of the same period: "I wish I was in print."

CHAPTER 10

Final Assessment

B Y THE measure of scholarly articles generated by American fiction writers of the twentieth century, Faulkner,
Hemingway, and Fitzgerald are the big three. Faulkner is
clearly the leader with 140 items in the 1974 Modern Language
Association International Bibliography; Hemingway has 78, and
Fitzgerald 47 (down from 59 in 1973). Faulkner, in fact, has
passed Melville (111), Henry James (94), Hawthorne (88), and
Mark Twain (61); and he leads all American writers in this
kind of popularity. Among all twentieth-century American writers,
poets and dramatists as well as novelists, T. S. Eliot (102),
Frost (76), and Pound (66) were the leaders.

Fifty years after the publication of *The Great Gatsby*, this is
select literary company for Fitzgerald to be in. By now, revival
of interest in his life and work is too solidly established to be
reversed. When Arthur Mizener's *The Far Side of Paradise* and
Alfred Kazin's *F. Scott Fitzgerald: The Man and His Work*
were published in 1951, these works marked the first resurgence
of interest in Fitzgerald after his death in 1940. *The Fitzgerald
Newsletter*, begun as a mimeographed sheet in 1958, had
developed into a hardcover *Fitzgerald/Hemingway Annual* by
1969. Its editor, Matthew J. Bruccoli, and many of the young
scholars published in the *Newsletter* mark a second phase of
interest in Fitzgerald's work, one which carried through into
the 1960's. Andrew Turnbull's biography in 1962 expanded the
details of the Fitzgeralds' lives, as did his publication of *Letters*
the following year.

With the 1970's, a broadening interest appeared in the increasing number of memoirs and articles devoted to Fitzgerald,
to the figures around him, or to his work. The women's movement helped focus attention on Zelda, the subject of Nancy
Milford's detailed biography in 1970; and many important details
of both Zelda's and Scott's personalities, backgrounds, and
relationships with others have emerged from recent books and

152

articles. Nonetheless, the continuing attention devoted to the Fitzgeralds' lives has not changed the basic picture that emerged in the major biographical works published in the 1950's and 1960's. Fitzgerald's story contributes more than most to the classic story of a boy from the provinces whose talents brought him fame and temporary fortune. That the story in the harsh fates of both Zelda and Scott seems to also carry a stern moral adds to its impact.

As the 1920's become more distant from us, the Fitzgeralds' lives cannot escape being affected by that distance. There has always been something mythic about them, and Fitzgerald's works are now experiencing a careful examination by critics drawn to the mythic in literature. Such criticism may arrive at a more successful merging of life and works than previous criticism. The legend of Fitzgerald's romantic life answers a need for an American mythic artist hero. Beneath that myth and woven into many of Fitzgerald's works are those myths of youth and beauty and destroying time, of searching and striving, of conflict between forces of good and evil which were the staples of fiction long before Fitzgerald arrived to make his own distinguished contribution.

After the 1960's, there has been little waning of interest in Fitzgerald's life and works. For the general public, the movie version of *The Great Gatsby*, with Robert Redford following Alan Ladd (1949) and Warner Baxter (1926) as Jay Gatsby, reached the widest audience. The television presentation, *Scott Fitzgerald in Hollywood*, followed a familiar pattern of covering the whole of Fitzgerald's career, though it ostensibly focused on his years in Hollywood. Previous television productions have included *The Great Gatsby*, *The Last Tycoon*, "The Last of the Belles," "Winter Dreams," and "The Rich Boy." The movie, *Tender Is the Night*, can still be seen occasionally on television. *The Last Tycoon* is in production as this chapter is being written.

Fitzgerald's work has also continued to be published and republished. Among the most interesting publications of the 1970's are the Bodley Head *Bits of Paradise* which contains eleven uncollected stories by Scott Fitzgerald and all of Zelda Fitzgerald's short stories, edited by Scottie Fitzgerald Smith and Matthew J. Bruccoli in 1973; Jackson Bryer and John Kuehl have edited and published *The Basil and Josephine Stories* (1973) and *F. Scott Fitzgerald: In His Own Time*, a collection of previously uncollected miscellaneous material by and about

Fitzgerald. The most recent reprint of a Fitzgerald work is Scribner's edition of his play, *The Vegetable*, which had been out of print since its first publication in 1923. Scribner's has kept all of Fitzgerald's novels and collections of short stories in print in paperbound editions. (*All the Sad Young Men* and *Tales of the Jazz Age* provided selections for *Six Tales of the Jazz Age and Other Stories.*) According to Matthew Bruccoli, sales of all of Fitzgerald's works published by Scribner's have increased from seventy-two copies in 1940, the year of his death, to a steady half million copies a year since 1966.

While much of this publishing has been in response to the general popularity of Fitzgerald and his work, Fitzgerald's reputation among scholars and critics is as strongly evidenced by a continuing flow of scholarly publications. Articles of substance written since the first edition of this book have been added to the selected bibliography at the end of this volume. In addition, Matthew Bruccoli's definitive bibliography, facsimile editions of the manuscript of *The Great Gatsby* and of *The Ledger*, and Scribner's handsomely produced edition of the *Scrapbooks* and *Notebooks* greatly extend the possibilities for examining Fitzgerald's practices and development as a writer.

Although Fitzgerald's life has long had a fascination not precisely tied to his literary standing, the number and quality of published biographical materials are of a kind accorded to only a few modern American authors. In addition to major biographies and critical studies, Fitzgerald's letters have been available in Turnbull's edition since 1963. Since that date, separate volumes have been published that bring together Fitzgerald's correspondence with his editor, his agent, and his daughter. The memoirs that continue to appear are of a mixed character; for, fairly considered, they satisfy curiosity more than they contribute to an assessment of his literary standing. Some, like Tony Buttitta's *After the Good Gay Times* (1974), make too much of a brief personal acquaintance. Others, like Sheilah Graham's *The Real Scott Fitzgerald* (1976), repeat some of what already is known but still contribute to our knowledge of Fitzgerald as a person and as a writer.

Even now, as in his lifetime, Fitzgerald appears as both a serious writer and a notable American figure identified with the popular fiction he wrote. His work continues to enjoy great favor, perhaps because he is less mannered than Hemingway, less demanding than Faulkner, and less ponderous than a dozen novelists in the Naturalistic tradition. He, Hemingway, and Faulkner are likely to remain the most interesting and rewarding of American fiction writers between the two World Wars.

I   A Review of Fitzgerald Criticism

Fitzgerald's present status should be set against his varying fortunes from the publication of his first book to the present. Alfred Kazin's collection of criticism, *F. Scott Fitzgerald, the Man and His Work* (World, 1951), provides a good many of the documents for that study.[1] The rest are to be found in the newspapers and magazines which reviewed Fitzgerald's works.

This Side of Paradise is such a part of the Fitzgerald legend that its success in 1920 is often exaggerated. Certainly it did well for a first novel, but its successful run was not a long one. Though it reached fourth place on the *Publishers' Weekly* best-seller list in July, 1920, it had dropped to eighth by September; by the next month, it had disappeared. Sinclair Lewis' *Main Street*, published the same year, was a top seller for sixteen months between 1920 and 1923. The attention given *This Side of Paradise* was the kind accorded to any number of novels and novelists in any year of publishing. In 1925, for example, the *New York Times Book Review* pointed out that by actual count among the better reviewers, there were 137 best novels of the year. What made *This Side of Paradise* stand out was Fitzgerald's simultaneous development as a writer of popular magazine fiction who was apparently living the very life he described.

By the time of the publication of *The Beautiful and Damned*, Fitzgerald's notoriety had increased greatly. Though the novel was reviewed more harshly, the harshness was usually tempered with mention of promising talent waiting to fulfill itself. Through almost all the reviews, the comments about the book were fewer than those about F. Scott Fitzgerald, the interpreter of the younger generation. The one notable exception was Edmund Wilson's essay in *The Bookman*, March, 1922.[2]

This review is so much to the point about Fitzgerald the writer that it might have been written from the perspective of seeing his entire career. "He has been given imagination without intellectual control of it . . ." Wilson's bluntest paragraph of criticism begins. Later in the essay, he emphasizes the salient points about Fitzgerald's work that all later critics needed to recognize: his feeling for the Middle West; the duality in his Irish temperament; the presence of gaiety and style in his work. Certainly, Fitzgerald paid attention throughout his career to what Wilson said and would continue to say.

The only other review of distinction written about Fitzgerald before *The Great Gatsby* was an essay by Paul Rosenfeld in 1924. Rosenfeld was, with Edmund Wilson, Mencken, and John Peale Bishop, a reviewer whom Fitzgerald respected. His review of Fitzgerald's stories and novels through *Tales of the Jazz Age* centers on the charge that "too oftentimes his good material eludes him." But, as if asking for what he was to get in *The Great Gatsby*, Rosenfeld concludes: "He has seen his material from its own point of view, and he has seen it completely from without. But he has never done what the artist does: seen it simultaneously from within and without; and loved it and judged it, too."[3] One conjectures that the essay might have been in Fitzgerald's mind when he wrote Edmund Wilson about *The Great Gatsby*: "I wonder what Rosenfeld thought of it?"

Considering the almost uniform praise it has received in the past decade, *The Great Gatsby* fared badly at the time of its publication. Fitzgerald was not merely being peevish when he wrote to John Peale Bishop, "Thank you for your most pleasant, full, discerning and helpful letter about *The Great Gatsby*. It is about the only criticism that the book has had which has been intelligible."[4] What may have been more discouraging than the reviews was the rapidity with which the book disappeared as a novel of unusual merit. Rebecca West, writing in *The Bookman* in 1928, was almost the only writer to turn back to *The Great Gatsby* in full appreciation of it between its publication and its inclusion in The Modern Library in 1934. Obviously, *The Great Gatsby* did not succeed in establishing Fitzgerald as an important writer in the ten years after its publication.

The miscellaneous work of 1925 to 1934 added little to Fitzgerald's reputation. It is not surprising that *Tender Is the Night* was reviewed either as a pathetic attempt to breathe life into material Fitzgerald had exhausted in the 1920's, or as a book which marked the reappearance of a writer long regarded as finished. The reviews were generally more unfavorable than the reviews of any other Fitzgerald novel.[5] Even the favorable reviews were disappointed that the novel was not better. The longer reviews, as could be expected, expended as many words in looking back upon Fitzgerald's career as in examining the novel at hand. But neither *Tender Is the Night* nor *Taps at*

Reveille provoked the kind of lengthy and serious examination of Fitzgerald's work which has become a commonplace since World War II.

Fitzgerald's death in 1940 and the publication of *The Last Tycoon* the next year stimulated a number of short but discerning observations about his work. Sentiment accounts for the almost entirely favorable reaction to *The Last Tycoon*, but the essays in *The New Republic* in 1941 by Malcolm Cowley and Glenway Wescott began to build the solid ground on which Fitzgerald's present reputation rests. The sales of *The Crack-Up* in 1945 caused *Publishers' Weekly* to hint at a Fitzgerald revival. Sometime between the beginning of World War II and its close, Fitzgerald began to return to popularity and to receive more critical attention.

The first serious articles to appear in a literary quarterly were the two in the *Virginia Quarterly Review*: "The Missing All," by John Peale Bishop (Winter, 1937),[6] and "Invite with Gilded Edges," by Charles Weir, Jr. (Winter, 1944). In 1945, Viking Press included Fitzgerald's work among their Portables, and that same year saw articles in *Partisan Review*, *The New Yorker*, *Commonweal*, *Accent*, and *The Yale Review*. The publication of *The Crack-Up* provided the occasion, but the essays were lengthier, more penetrating, and more affectionate than called for by the ordinary review. From that time on, the Fitzgerald revival moved briskly along, the "revival" itself becoming the specific subject for articles in *The Kenyon Review* (Summer, 1951), *The Freeman* (November 5, 1951), *South Atlantic Quarterly* (January, 1955), and *The Australian Quarterly* (June, 1957).

The growth of literary scholarship both in America and abroad is a phenomenon of the 1960's, and scholarly attention to Fitzgerald probably owes as much to the general growth of academic publishing as to specific rising interest in Fitzgerald. Kazin's collection of critical articles in 1951 was followed by Arthur Mizener's *F. Scott Fitzgerald: A Collection of Critical Essays* (1963) and by my own *F. Scott Fitzgerald: Contemporary Studies in Literature* (1973). *The Great Gatsby* itself occasioned a collection of critical articles edited by Ernest Lockridge (1968) and two research anthologies. It seems fair to say that criticism of Fitzgerald through the 1960's was uncommonly interesting. Fitzgerald's work seems to provoke other writers into responding to it, and good critics continue to be attracted to his work out of respect for his prose style and storyteller's art. As more and more criticism has accumulated (over 1500 articles have been published about him and his work since 1941), it is not surprising to find that many recent articles are concerned with small matters and that more substantial efforts may consist of subjecting a Fitzgerald work to some currently fashionable critical technique or bias. As we have noted, the women's movement has justifiably revived an interest in Zelda and her work (*Save Me the Waltz* is once more easily available), just as an attention to myth has provoked articles which see Fitzgerald's works from a particularly illuminating perspective.

The Great Gatsby continues to draw the greatest amount of critical attention. That novel's stature has steadily increased since the 1950's, and its continuing sales have been phenomenal— 3,500,000 copies in Scribner's editions alone. Among foreign critics, Fitzgerald has aroused less interest than has either Hemingway or Faulkner; but his reputation is nevertheless international. *The Great Gatsby* again leads the list of his translated works, having been translated into thirty-three languages. Although Sergio Perosa's *L'Arte di F. Scott Fitzgerald* (1960; translated 1965) is the only non-English critical book of which I am aware, Fitzgerald's novels and stories have been translated into most of the world's major languages, and a body of critical work is beginning to appear in Japan, India, and the European countries in which there is a strong interest in American literature.

II *Final Appraisal*

By now, the solid claim upon which Fitzgerald's reputation is based have been made by dozens of critics who have also recognized his weaknesses. Almost from the beginning of serious interest in Fitzgerald, he was praised as a social historian of his time and of the upper middle class. He has, moreover, been accorded more respect in recent years for the breadth and depth of his view. Few critics fail to recognize that his attempt to define "the rich" was a legitimate and peculiarly appropriate subject for an American writer. Nor is it often urged now that he was unable to see the subject clearly because the sight of money distorted his vision. Money and American manners are inextricably linked. The literary respectability of the novel of manners has increased since the 1930's, and Fitzgerald has been placed with Edith Wharton and Henry James as a very shrewd observer of American society.

Second, Fitzgerald's subconscious awareness of American values has been increasingly emphasized in recent criticism. *The Great Gatsby* has been separated from the specifics of Jazz Age life on Long Island and has become a profound commentary upon modern America as a descendant of a romantic, frontier past in which idealism is as strong a component as materialism. In Gatsby, in Anthony Patch, in Dick Diver, Fitzgerald has questioned the adequacy of present America to sustain its heroic past. More than that, in his "fable of East and West," Fitzgerald has opposed the American past and present in terms of the creation of a contemporary ethic in the pastoral West and the debasement of that ethic in the industrial East.

Third, Fitzgerald's moral awareness has enhanced his claim to be taken seriously as a novelist. *The Great Gatsby* is the central novel of the 1920's to assert a staunch moral point of view based on a sense of "fundamental decencies" against a morality based solely on power and position. Despite the pessimism and determinism which run through his work, Fitzgerald still sees man as capable not only of choice but of a vision superior to what he himself may be. Few readers can escape the effect of the "ordering" of his novels which comes from his strong moral sense. There is little of the naturalist in Fitzgerald's treatment of character, and his reputation probably profits from his disconnection from literary naturalism and his hewing to the moral line which runs through the best American writing.

Fourth, the immediacy of Fitzgerald's writing has not vanished with the passing of time. Though many of his popular stories have gained favor by the nostalgia they now create for the most colorful period of the recent past, they have also gained because he re-created the past with extraordinary clarity. Whether a reader responds with the instinctive passion for that which can be seen, felt, and heard, or is impressed with the way Fitzgerald's particulars evoke a larger reality, he arrives at a respect for Fitzgerald's ability to make a time, a place, a person, "live."

Fifth, and related to the above, Fitzgerald's style impresses any reader with more than a passing interest in writing. One of the contributions of recent scholarship is to make widely available manuscript materials which show the care with which Fitzgerald fashioned phrase and sentence and paragraph. *The*

Great Gatsby manuscript and "The Note-Books," published in Edmund Wilson's *The Crack-Up*, shed much light about how Fitzgerald worked. The movement and clarity of his sentences, the aptness of his phrases, and the poetic quality of his prose are marks of his style. Even his poor stories are often partially redeemed by sentences or paragraphs of excellent writing. Sustained throughout a novel, as in *The Great Gatsby*, or in a section, as in the Rosemary section of *Tender Is the Night*, Fitzgerald's style reaches that excellence few prose writers and not many more poets ever reach. Moreover, the style is in the mainstream of English literary development; it impresses, not because it is intensely original or eccentric, but because it is a graceful, lucid, and highly evocative prose almost as easily connected with Dryden as with Joseph Conrad.

Finally, and no small virtue, Fitzgerald is a good storyteller, though not in the same sense that Sherwood Anderson is a good teller of tales. Rather, Fitzgerald is a storyteller concerned not only with the story as "life" or "truth" but the story as "art." This fact is easily lost sight of in the hundred or so stories turned out for the popular magazines and in the numerous retellings of the same basic stories. But, despite both of these detractions, Fitzgerald's fiction is replete with stories interesting in themselves and artfully put down. If he narrates or is concerned with only one story—Fitzgerald claimed writers really have only one— it is a story turned around and around to see it from this side and that so that one listens again and again. Though he liked to think of himself as a novelist (perhaps for somewhat the same reasons as his dream of himself as a rich man), his novels are often weaker in total effect than the stories of which they are made. The short story was obviously congenial to his temperament as a writer, and it may well be that his short stories will be the supporting evidence—*The Great Gatsby* is Exhibit A—of his lasting claim to attention.

It is worth adding that there is joy in Fitzgerald's work that should not be ignored when dwelling upon profundities, complexities, and tragic implications. Edmund Wilson early described this joyous characteristic as a "quality exceedingly rare among even the young American writers of the day: he is almost the only one among them who has any real lighthearted gaiety."[7] Recognizing that quality and acknowledging its worth may draw attention to the variety to be found in a writer who is commonly charged with having had a narrow range. It also adds to the dimensions of *The Great Gatsby* and *Tender Is the Night*, those novels that do most to maintain Fitzgerald's reputation as a serious writer. Not only theme and technique distinguish these novels, but flashes of brilliance, comic as well as tragic, illuminate individual scenes.

His weaknesses are obvious. His range is narrow; his works of great excellence also few. The tragic view often results in the merely pathetic effect. Sentimentality mars his poor work and threatens his best work. The surface is often so shimmering that it conceals the depths—and the lack of depth—beneath. His style is admirable; but, though Fitzgerald claimed to see a stamp set upon all he wrote, it lacks the distinctive qualities which make Hemingway's style an influential one and which make Faulkner's capable of such powerful effects. At its worst, Fitzgerald's style shades off into fine writing; when practiced casually, into competent but undistinguished prose. He is too lucid in unimportant matters and too divided when writing most seriously to achieve a high, serious art. "Waste" is the pejorative term which defines his life and work—waste of talent, and waste of situations, characters, and feelings on writing done to make possible the wasted hours of his life. Finally his work is uninformed by any philosophy other than that residing in a youthful romanticism he could never abandon.

These strictures are not sufficient to disallow Fitzgerald's claim to a distinguished place in modern American writing. Above all, he has the strong alliance of the amateur reader and the professional literary man—student, scholar, and writer—to keep his reputation secure. For he seldom failed to live up to that sole obligation which Henry James said we should require of the novel—that it be interesting. And he never failed to be aware of his own observation about his contemporaries: "that material, however closely observed, is as elusive as the moment in which it has its existence unless it is purified by an incorruptible style and by the catharsis of a passionate emotion."[8]

Notes and References

Preface

1. "Scott Fitzgerald's Fable of East and West," in *F. Scott Fitzgerald*, ed. Kenneth Eble (New York, 1973), p. 66.

2. Edmund Wilson, ed., *The Crack-Up* (New York, 1945), p. 298.

3. Edmund Wilson, "Thoughts on Being Bibliographed," *The Princeton University Library Chronicle*, V (February, 1944), p. 54.

4. Kenneth Eble, *F. Scott Fitzgerald* (New York, 1963), p. 8.

Chapter One

1. Grace Flandrau, "Saint Paul: The Untamable Twin," in *The Taming of the Frontier*, ed. Duncan Aikman (New York, 1925), p. 152. See also the American Guide Series, *Minnesota* (New York, 1938), "But by that time [the 1870's] St. Paul, with 62 jobbing firms and a wholesale grocery larger than any in Chicago was absorbed in its dream of becoming the great railroad center of freight transfer and distribution for all of northwest America . . . ," p. 209.

2. F. Scott Fitzgerald's Scrapbook, Princeton University Library.

3. Andrew Turnbull, *Scott Fitzgerald* (New York: 1962), p. 281.

4. *The Princeton University Library Chronicle*, XII, No. 4 (Summer, 1951), 187. Henry Dan Piper, "F. Scott Fitzgerald and the Image of His Father," *ibid.*, pp. 181–86, makes a detailed study of the close relationship between father and son.

5. See Henry Dan Piper, "Scott Fitzgerald's Prep-School Writings," *The Princeton University Library Chronicle*, XVII, No. 1 (Autumn, 1955), 1–10. Fitzgerald's first story, "The Mystery of the Raymond Mortgage," has recently been reprinted in a limited edition by Random House, 1961; it may also be found in *Ellery Queen's 15th Mystery Annual*.

6. "Early Success," in *The Crack-Up*, ed. Edmund Wilson (New York, 1945), p. 85.

7. Scrapbook.

8. Fitzgerald's Ledger, part of the Fitzgerald collection in the Princeton University Library and now available in a facsimile edition, furnishes numerous correspondences between events of Fitzgerald's youth and the Basil Duke Lee stories.

9. "The Note-Books," in *The Crack-Up*, p. 95.

10. Turnbull, pp. 66–68.

11. Like so much in Fitzgerald's fiction, even this name came in part from his past. One of the new boys elected to Cottage Club at the same time as Fitzgerald was named "Labouisse."

12. *This Side of Paradise* (Dell Edition, D140), pp. 160–61. This passage first appeared as a poem, "Princeton, the Last Day," *The Nassau Literary Magazine* (May, 1917). A parody of it is part of "Paradise Be Damned!" by F. Scott Fitzjazzer, in Christopher Ward, *The Triumph of the Nut* (New York, 1923), pp. 105–18.

Chapter Two

1. Arthur Mizener, *The Far Side of Paradise* (Boston, 1951), p. 39.

2. Edmund Wilson, ed., *The Crack-Up* (New York, 1945), p. 211.

3. Christian Gauss, "Edmund Wilson, the Campus, and the Nassau 'Lit,' " *The Princeton University Library Chronicle*, V (February, 1944), 54.

4. *This Side of Paradise* (Dell Edition, D140), p. 125.

5. Edmund Wilson, "Thoughts on Being Bibliographed," *The Princeton University Library Chronicle*, V (February, 1944), 54.

6. It hardly needs stating that Fitzgerald's low grades were not the result of inability, though his comparatively good grades in English and philosophy support Andrew Turnbull's judgment that "Fitzgerald's gift was narrowly, concentratedly verbal." When he took his army tests in 1917, he scored 92.25 in English and American literature, 85 in general history, and 77.5 in French.

7. "My Lost City," in *The Crack-Up*, p. 24.

8. Fitzgerald's early reading tastes are not far from those of the Princeton class of 1916. The favorite fiction writers were Tarkington, Churchill, Scott, Kipling, and Dickens; favorite poets were Tennyson, Service, Kipling, and Ella Wheeler Wilcox. *Ivanhoe* was the favorite novel; "Crossing the Bar" was the favorite poem.

9. *The Crack-Up*, p. 246.

10. "Who's Who—And Why," *Saturday Evening Post* (September 18, 1920), p. 61.

11. Letter to Maxwell Perkins, April 23, 1938.

12. Mizener, pp. 147–48.

13. It is instructive to compare this section of *This Side of Paradise* with the original story in the *Nassau Lit*. The heightened emotion which is often irritating in its misty excesses was added in Fitzgerald's rewriting of the original. The diction is much improved; the feeling is greatly but not always successfully intensified.

14. As further illustration of how Fitzgerald's miscellaneous writing flows into stories and novels, consider the parallel between the passage cited and one he wrote in 1917 for a review of Shane Leslie's *The Celt and the World*. Fitzgerald quotes from memory from Leslie's book: "the end of one era and the beginning of another to which no Gods have as yet been rash enough to give their names."

15. In The Ledger, p. 172, he marked 1917 as "Last year as a Catholic."

Chapter Three

1. "Early Success," in *The Crack-Up*, ed. Edmund Wilson (New York, 1945), pp. 85–90; first appeared in *American Cavalcade* (October, 1937).

2. *Ibid.*, pp. 89–90.

3. Zelda Fitzgerald, *Save Me the Waltz* (London, 1953), p. 270.

4. Arthur Mizener, *The Far Side of Paradise* (Boston, 1951), Footnote 11, p. 323.

5. *Ibid.*, Footnote 51, p. 325.

6. The collections of so-called "Best" stories were particularly drawn to these serious stories which neither Fitzgerald nor later readers regarded highly. Of these early stories, the *O'Brien Best Short Stories* reprinted "Two for a Cent" and gave high ratings to "The Cut-Glass Bowl" and "The Four Fists." The O. Henry collection also awarded "The Cut-Glass Bowl" a high rating.

7. A close study of modern American fiction, Austin M. Wright's *The American Short Story in the Twenties* (Chicago, 1961), repeatedly stresses the "old-fashioned" character of Fitzgerald's stories as compared with those of Sherwood Anderson, Hemingway, Faulkner, and Katherine Anne Porter—the other modern writers under consideration.

8. *The Crack-Up*, p. 180.

9. Introduction, *Six Tales of the Jazz Age and Other Stories* (New York, 1960).

10. "What I Think and Feel at Twenty-Five," *American Magazine* (September, 1922), p. 16.

Chapter Four

1. "How to Live on $36,000 a Year," *Saturday Evening Post* (April 5, 1924), reprinted in Arthur Mizener, ed., *Afternoon of an Author* (New York, 1958) together with the companion essay, "How to Live on Practically Nothing a Year," *Saturday Evening Post* (September 20, 1924).

2. "My Lost City," in *The Crack-Up*, ed. Edmund Wilson (New York, 1945), p. 29.

3. "Early Success," in *The Crack-Up*, p. 87.

4. *The Crack-Up*, p. 173.

5. "Wait Till You Have Children of Your Own!" *Woman's Home Companion* (July, 1924), p. 13.

6. Arthur Mizener, *The Far Side of Paradise* (Boston, 1951), p. 142.

7. "The Literary Spotlight—VI: F. Scott Fitzgerald," *The Bookman*, LV (March, 1922), pp. 20–25.

8. "Two for a Cent," *The Metropolitan Magazine* (April, 1922), p. 24.

9. *The Crack-Up*, p. 101.

10. Marius Bewley, *The Eccentric Design* (London, 1959), p. 260.

11. Maxwell Perkins wrote Fitzgerald a close analysis of the similarities between "Of Thee I Sing" and "The Vegetable"; he concluded that the differences were so many and so obvious that there was little chance of supporting a claim of infringement.

Chapter Five

1. Edmund Wilson, ed., *The Crack-Up* (New York, 1945), p. 264.

2. Reprinted in *The Crack-Up*, pp. 34–40.

3. See James E. Miller, Jr., *The Fictional Technique of Scott Fitzgerald* (The Hague, 1957), pp. 79–81; John Kuehl, "Scott Fitzgerald's Reading," *The Princeton University Library Chronicle*, XXII, No. 2 (Winter, 1961), 58–89; Robert W. Stallman, "Conrad and *The Great Gatsby*," *Twentieth Century Literature*, I (April, 1955), 5–12.

4. "Minnesota's Capital in the Role of Main Street," *The Literary Digest International Book Review* (March, 1923), pp. 35–36.

5. "Under Fire," *The Literary Review of the New York Evening Post* (May 26, 1923), p. 715.

6. Charles C. Baldwin, *The Men Who Make Our Novels* (New York, 1924), p. 167.

7. "Introduction," *The Great Gatsby* (Modern Library edition, 1934), pp. ix–x.

8. Letter to Maxwell Perkins, July, 1922.

9. Many of Fitzgerald's best efforts were achieved by reworking or re-ordering his material. This final arresting image was originally written as the conclusion of Chapter One. By the time he had finished his corrected first draft, he recognized that it would provide an effective conclusion and transposed it with very few changes to the final page.

10. The remarks about the revisions on the galley proofs are based upon my study of the galleys in the Fitzgerald collection at Princeton University and now available in a facsimile edition.

11. *The Great Gatsby* (The Scribner Library Edition), p. 108.

12. *Ibid.*, pp. 66–67. The most celebrated of Fitzgerald's afterthoughts in composing *The Great Gatsby* is probably that concerning Dr. Eckleburg's eyes. As Arthur Mizener has recounted that incident, Fitzgerald did not create the symbol until he saw a dust jacket which "intended to suggest by two enormous eyes Daisy brooding over an amusement park version of New York." He wrote to Maxwell Perkins: "For Christ's sake don't give anyone that jacket you're saving for me. I've written it into the book." Mizener, p. 170.

13. *The Great Gatsby*, p. 129. This whole scene, a vital one, was extensively revised in the galleys. The material about Biloxi, for example, was added at that time.

14. *Ibid.*, p. 138.
15. *The Crack-Up*, p. 269.

Chapter Six

1. Edmund Wilson, ed., *The Crack-Up* (New York, 1945), pp. 89–90.
2. "The Moral of Scott Fitzgerald," *New Republic*, CIV (February 17, 1941), 213–17. Reprinted in *The Crack-Up*, pp. 323–37.
3. Reprinted in Arthur Mizener, ed., *Afternoon of an Author* (New York, 1958), pp. 117–22.
4. *The Crack-Up*, pp. 272. The spellings are Fitzgerald's.
5. "Show Mr. and Mrs. F. to Number ——," *Esquire* (May; June, 1934). Reprinted in *The Crack-Up*, p. 41.

Chapter Seven

1. Arthur Mizener, *The Far Side of Paradise* (Boston, 1951), Footnote 15, p. 327.
2. *Ibid.*, Footnote 30, p. 324.
3. Dwight Taylor, *Joy Ride* (New York, 1959), pp. 234–50.
4. Fitzgerald frequently endows more than one character in a story or novel with his own character traits. Nick Carraway and Jay Gatsby in *The Great Gatsby*, and Anthony Patch and Richard Caramel in *The Beautiful and Damned*, are the best examples.

Chapter Eight

1. Andrew Turnbull, *Scott Fitzgerald* (New York, 1962), pp. 206–208.
2. Arthur Mizener, *The Far Side of Paradise* (New York, 1951), p. 228.
3. Turnbull, pp. 209–40.
4. Matthew Bruccoli, *The Composition of Tender Is the Night* (Pittsburgh, 1963), brings all this material together for the first time.
5. Mizener, pp. 307–308.
6. Matthew Bruccoli, "*Tender Is the Night* and the Reviewers," *Modern Fiction Studies*, VII, No. 1 (Spring, 1961), 49–54.
7. William Troy, "The Perfect Life," *Nation* (April 17, 1935), pp. 454–56.

Chapter Nine

1. Arthur Mizener, ed., *Afternoon of an Author* (New York, 1958), p. 189.

2. Arthur Mizener, *The Far Side of Paradise* (New York, 1951), p. 263.

3. Edmund Wilson, ed., *The Crack-Up* (New York, 1945), p. 232.

4. *Ibid.*, p. 298.

5. Andrews Wanning, "Fitzgerald and His Brethren," reprinted in *F. Scott Fitzgerald: The Man and His Work*, ed. Alfred Kazin (Cleveland and New York, 1951), p. 166.

6. Kazin, p. 211.

Chapter Ten

1. The collection, however, is somewhat misleading in dating the essays by the date of their inclusion in book form rather than by the date of their first appearance. It is important to a close study of Fitzgerald's development as a writer and personality to know that Edmund Wilson's "The Delegate from Great Neck" appeared April 30, 1924 (*New Republic*), not 1926, and that Wilson's "Spotlight" in *The Bookman* appeared in 1922, not 1925.

2. "The Literary Spotlight—VI: F. Scott Fitzgerald," *The Bookman*, LV (March, 1922), 20–25. Reprinted in Kazin, pp. 77–83.

3. Paul Rosenfeld, *Men Seen: Twenty-Four Modern Authors* (New York, 1925), pp. 215–24. Reprinted in Kazin, pp. 71–76, and in *The Crack-Up*, pp. 317–22.

4. *The Crack-Up*, p. 271.

5. Matthew Bruccoli, "*Tender Is the Night* and the Reviewers," *Modern Fiction Studies*, VII, No. 1 (Spring, 1961), 49–54.

6. It is indicative of Fitzgerald's state at the time of this article and after that he regarded it as an attack upon him: "a nice return for ten years of trying to set him up in a literary way," he wrote in 1940.

7. Edmund Wilson, "Fitzgerald before *The Great Gatsby*," in Kazin, p. 82.

8. "How to Waste Material: A Note on My Generation," *The Bookman* (May, 1926), reprinted in *Afternoon of an Author*, ed. Arthur Mizener (New York, 1958), p. 120.

Selected Bibliography

PRIMARY SOURCES

1. Novels and Plays

This Side of Paradise. New York: Scribner's, 1920.
The Beautiful and Damned. New York: Scribner's, 1922.
The Vegetable, or From President to Postman. New York: Scribner's, 1923.
The Great Gatsby. New York: Scribner's, 1925.
Tender Is the Night. New York: Scribner's, 1934.
The Last Tycoon. Ed. by Edmund Wilson. New York: Scribner's, 1941.

2. Stories and Articles

Flappers and Philosophers. New York: Scribner's, 1921. ("The Offshore Pirate," "The Ice Palace," "Head and Shoulders," "The Cut-Glass Bowl," "Bernice Bobs Her Hair," "Benediction," "Dalyrimple Goes Wrong," "The Four Fists.")
Tales of the Jazz Age. New York: Scribner's, 1922. ("The Jelly-Bean," "The Camel's Back," "May Day," "Porcelain and Pink," "The Diamond as Big as the Ritz," "The Curious Case of Benjamin Button," "Tarquin of Cheapside," "O Russet Witch!" "The Lees of Happiness," "Mr. Icky," "Jemina.")
All the Sad Young Men. New York: Scribner's, 1926. ("The Rich Boy," "Winter Dreams," "The Baby Party," "Absolution," "Rags Martin-Jones and the Pr-nce of W-les," "The Adjuster," "Hot and Cold Blood," "The Sensible Thing," "Gretchen's Forty Winks.")
Taps at Reveille. New York: Scribner's, 1935. (Basil Duke Lee stories: "The Scandal Detectives," "The Freshest Boy," "He Thinks He's Wonderful," "The Captured Shadow," "The Perfect Life"; Josephine stories: "First Blood," "A Nice Quiet Place," "A Woman with a Past"; and "Crazy Sunday," "Two Wrongs," "The Night of Chancellorsville," "The Last of the Belles," "Majesty," "Family in the Wind," "A Short Trip Home," "One Interne," "The Fiend," "Babylon Revisited.")
Afternoon of an Author; A Selection of Uncollected Stories and Essays. Introduction and Notes by Arthur Mizener. New York: Scribner's, 1958. (Basil Duke Lee stories: "A Night at the Fair," "Forging Ahead," "Basil and Cleopatra,"; "Outside the Cabinet-

Maker's," "One Trip Abroad," "I Didn't Get Over," "Afternoon of an Author," "Design in Plaster"; Pat Hobby stories: "Boil Some Water—Lots of It," "Teamed with Genius," "No Harm Trying"; and "News of Paris—Fifteen Years Ago," "Princeton," "Who's Who—and Why," "How to Live on $36,000 a Year," "How to Live on Practically Nothing a Year," "How to Waste Material: A Note on My Generation," "Ten Years in the Advertising Business," "One Hundred False Starts," "Author's House.")

The Stories of F. Scott Fitzgerald. Introduction by Malcolm Cowley. New York: Scribner's, 1951. (Contains twenty-eight stories and these previously uncollected stories: "Magnetism," "The Rough Crossing," "The Bridal Party," "An Alcoholic Case," "The Long Way Out," "Financing Finnegan," "Pat Hobby Himself: A Patriotic Short, Two Old Timers," "Three Hours Between Planes," "The Lost Decade.")

The Pat Hobby Stories. Introduction by Arnold Gingrich. New York: Scribner's, 1962.

Babylon Revisited and Other Stories. New York: Scribner's, 1960. ("The Ice Palace," "May Day," "Absolution," "The Rich Boy," "The Diamond as Big as the Ritz," "Winter Dreams," "The Freshest Boy," "Babylon Revisited," "Crazy Sunday," "The Long Way Out.")

All of the above are available in paperbound editions published by Scribner's with the exception of *Tales of the Jazz Age* and *All the Sad Young Men,* the best of which have been brought into a new paperbound edition, *Six Tales of the Jazz Age and Other Stories,* Introduction by Frances Fitzgerald Lanahan. Scribner's has also issued an Omnibus Edition, *Three Novels of F. Scott Fitzgerald: The Great Gatsby,* Introduction by Malcolm Cowley; *Tender Is the Night* (with the Author's Final Revisions), edited by Malcolm Cowley; and *The Last Tycoon, An Unfinished Novel,* edited by Edmund Wilson; and *The Fitzgerald Reader,* edited by Arthur Mizener, both available in paperbound editions.

In addition, the following collections of original Fitzgerald writings are also available:

The Crack-Up. Edited by Edmund Wilson. New York: New Directions, 1945. ("Echoes of the Jazz Age," "My Lost City," "Ring," " 'Show Mr. and Mrs. F. to Number ——,' " "Auction—Model 1934," "Sleeping and Waking," "The Crack-Up," "Handle with Care," "Pasting It Together," "Early Success," "The Note-Books"; Letters.)

The Apprentice Fiction of F. Scott Fitzgerald, 1909–1917. Edited and Introduction by John Kuehl. New Brunswick, N. J.: Rutgers University Press, 1965.

The Basil and Joephine Stories. Edited and Introduction by John Kuehl and Jackson Bryer. New York: Scribner's, 1973.

Bits of Paradise: 21 Uncollected Stories by F. Scott & Zelda Fitzgerald. Edited by Scottie Fitzgerald Smith and Matthew J. Bruccoli with Foreword by Scottie Fitzgerald Smith. London: Bodley Head, 1973; New York: Scribner's, 1974.

The Bodley Head Scott Fitzgerald. 6 Vols. London: Bodley Head, 1958–1963.

F. Scott Fitzgerald: In His Own Time. Edited by Matthew J. Bruccoli and Jackson Bryer. Kent, Ohio: Kent State University Press, 1971. Reprinted Popular Library, 1974.

"The Great Gatsby": A Facsimile of the Manuscript. Washington, D. C.: NCR/Microcard Editions, 1973.

The Mystery of the Raymond Mortgage. New York: Random House, 1960.

The Portable F. Scott Fitzgerald. Selected by Dorothy Parker and Introduction by John O'Hara. New York: Viking, 1949.

Thoughtbook of Francis Scott Key Fitzgerald. Introduction by John Kuehl. Princeton: Princeton University Library, 1965.

3. Letters and Autobiographical Sources

As Ever, Scott Fitzgerald. Edited by Matthew J. Bruccoli and Jennifer McCabe Atkinson. Philadelphia: Lippincott, 1972. Correspondence with agent Harold Ober.

Dear Scott/Dear Max: the Fitzgerald-Perkins Correspondence. Edited by John Kuehl and Jackson Bryer. New York: Scribner's, 1971.

The Letters of F. Scott Fitzgerald. Edited by Andrew Turnbull. New York: Scribner's, 1963; London: Bodley Head, 1964.

Letters to His Daughter. Introduction by Frances Fitzgerald Lanahan. New York: Scribner's, 1965.

The Romantic Egoists: A Pictorial Autobiography from the Scrapbooks and Albums of Scott and Zelda Fitzgerald. Edited by Matthew J. Bruccoli, Scottie Fitzgerald Smith, and Joan P. Kerr. New York: Scribner's, 1974.

SECONDARY SOURCES

1. Bibliographies and Checklists

BEEBE, MAURICE and JACKSON R. BRYER. "Criticism of F. Scott Fitzgerald: A Selected Checklist," *Modern Fiction Studies*, VII (Spring, 1961), 82–94.

BRUCCOLI, MATTHEW J. *Checklist of F. Scott Fitzgerald.* Columbus, Ohio: Charles E. Merrill, 1970.

––––––. *F. Scott Fitzgerald: A Descriptive Bibliography.* Pittsburgh: University of Pittsburgh Press, 1972.

—————. *Fitzgerald Newsletter*, 1958–68. Washington, D. C.: Reprinted NCR/Microcard Editions, 1969.

BRUCCOLI, MATTHEW J. and C. E. FRAZER CLARK, JR. *Fitzgerald/ Hemingway Annual*. Washington, D. C.: NCR/Microcard Editions, 1969–

BRYER, JACKSON R. *The Critical Reputation of F. Scott Fitzgerald*. New Haven, Conn.: Archon, 1967.

—————. "F. Scott Fitzgerald," in *Sixteen Modern American Authors: A Survey of Research and Criticism*. Durham, N. C.: Duke University Press, 1973; New York: Norton, 1975.

PIPER, HENRY DAN. "F. Scott Fitzgerald: A Check List," *The Princeton University Library Chronicle*, XII (Summer, 1951), 196–208.

PORTER, BERNARD H. "The First Publications of F. Scott Fitzgerald," *Twentieth Century Literature*, V (January, 1960), 176–82.

2.   Biographical Works and Memoirs

BUTTITTA, TONY. *After the Good Gay Times: Asheville–Summer of '35/ A Season with F. Scott Fitzgerald*. New York: Viking, 1974. The authenticity of this memoir is questionable both in what the author purports to recall and emphasize forty years later and in the supposedly word-for-word conversations he reports having had with Fitzgerald.

GRAHAM, SHEILAH. *College of One*. New York: Viking, 1967.

—————. *The Rest of the Story*. New York: Coward-McCann, 1964.

—————. *The Real F. Scott Fitzgerald*. New York: Grosset & Dunlap, 1976. All of these publications add to our knowledge of Fitzgerald as writer and person as revealed in his relationship with Sheilah Graham in the years just before his death.

GRAHAM, SHEILAH and GEROLD FRANK. *Beloved Infidel*. New York: Holt, Rinehart & Winston, 1958. The first and least successful version of the Fitzgerald-Graham relationship.

MAYFIELD, SARA. *Exiles from Paradise: Zelda and Scott Fitzgerald*. New York: Delacorte Press, 1971. Strongly on Zelda Sayre's side in assigning praise and blame to the course of the Fitzgeralds' marriage, this memoir still adds much to our knowledge of the Fitzgeralds.

MILFORD, NANCY. *Zelda*. New York: Harper & Row, 1970. Excellent biography, tends to favor Zelda's point of view.

MIZENER, ARTHUR. *The Far Side of Paradise*. Boston: Houghton Mifflin, 1951. Revised edition 1965. National Book Award winner in its first publication; still the best combination of biography and critical study of Fitzgerald and his work.

PIPER, HENRY DAN. *F. Scott Fitzgerald/ A Critical Portrait*. New York: Holt, Rinehart & Winston, 1965. This study suffers somewhat from being a long time in preparation and from coming into publication after other books had covered the same ground.

TURNBULL, ANDREW. *Scott Fitzgerald.* New York: Scribner's, 1962. The most thorough biography which has the advantages not only of the author's personal acquaintance with Fitzgerald when Turnbull was growing up but also Turnbull's professional competence as a biographer.

3. Books

BRUCCOLI, MATTHEW J. *Apparatus for F. Scott Fitzgerald's The Great Gatsby.* Columbia: University of South Carolina Press, 1974.
—————. *The Composition of Tender Is the Night.* Pittsburgh: University of Pittsburgh Press, 1963. Both of these books are very useful guides to a close study of these two novels.
—————. *Profile of F. Scott Fitzgerald.* Columbus, Ohio: Charles E. Merrill, 1971. Good, short sketch of Fitzgerald's life and career.
CALLAHAN, JOHN F. *The Illusions of a Nation: Myth and History in the Novels of F. Scott Fitzgerald.* Urbana: University of Illinois Press, 1972. This academic book does some limiting and distorting of Fitzgerald's work to make it fit the author's thesis.
COWLEY, MALCOLM and ROBERT COWLEY, eds. *Fitzgerald and the Jazz Age.* New York: Scribner's, 1966. This book, like others of Cowley, benefits from Cowley's own notable literary career in the 1920's and 1930's.
CROSLAND, ANDREW. *Concordance to The Great Gatsby.* Detroit: Gale Research, 1975. The last word in homage to *The Great Gatsby* as a sacred text.
CROSS, K. G. W. *Scott Fitzgerald.* Edinburgh and London: Oliver & Boyd, 1964; New York: Barnes & Noble, 1966. Short, useful critical study.
EBLE, KENNETH E., ed. *F. Scott Fitzgerald: A Collection of Criticism.* New York: McGraw-Hill, 1973. Selects materials which were published in the 1960's and 1970's and which are not found in previous collections.
FITZGERALD, ZELDA. *Save Me the Waltz.* New York: Scribners, 1932. Introduction by Harry T. Moore, Carbondale: Southern Illinois University Press, 1967; New American Library, 1972. In many ways the Fitzgeralds' familiar story told from Zelda's perspective.
GOLDHURST, WILLIAM. *F. Scott Fitzgerald and His Contemporaries.* Cleveland and New York: World, 1963. Though a reader might quarrel with the author's critical judgments, he presents a useful bringing together of writers linked with Fitzgerald in one way or another.
HIGGINS, JOHN A. *F. Scott Fitzgerald: A Study of the Stories.* Jamaica, N. Y.: St. John's University Press, 1971. May contain more than most readers want to know about Fitzgerald's stories.

HINDUS, MILTON. *F. Scott Fitzgerald: An Introduction and Interpretation.* New York: Holt, Rinehart & Winston, 1968. Probably the least successful of the short guides to Fitzgerald's life and works.

HOFFMAN, FREDERICK J., ed. *The Great Gatsby: A Study.* New York: Scribner's, 1962. Compiled when "sourcebooks" were in flower, this collection brings together much interesting material that bears upon the novel.

KAZIN, ALFRED, ed. *F. Scott Fitzgerald: The Man and His Work.* Cleveland and New York: World, 1951. Earliest collection of critical appraisals of Fitzgerald's work; still useful for material published during his lifetime.

LaHOOD, MARVIN J., ed. *Tender Is the Night: Essays in Criticism.* Bloomington: Indiana University Press, 1969. Much of the mixed character of this novel comes through in the mixed responses of critics to it.

LATHAM, AARON. *Crazy Sundays. F. Scott Fitzgerald in Hollywood.* New York: Viking, 1970. Interesting, thorough account of Fitzgerald's various attempts to function as a screenwriter.

LEHAN, RICHARD D. *F. Scott Fitzgerald and the Craft of Fiction.* Carbondale: Southern Illinois University Press, 1966. Strains here and there but a useful complement to Miller's generally more impressive study.

LOCKRIDGE, ERNEST, ed. *Twentieth Century Interpretations of The Great Gatsby.* Englewood Cliffs, N. J.: Prentice-Hall, 1968. Though much more has been written about this novel since publication of this collection, it still contains major critical studies.

MILLER, JAMES E., JR. *The Fictional Technique of F. Scott Fitzgerald.* The Hague: Nijhoff, 1957. Enlarged edition—*F. Scott Fitzgerald: His Art and His Technique.* New York: New York University Press, 1964. Best single study of Fitzgerald's distinction as a writer of fiction.

MIZENER, ARTHUR, ed. *F. Scott Fitzgerald: A Collection of Critical Essays.* Englewood Cliffs, N. J.: Prentice-Hall, 1963. Supplements Kazin's earlier collection with critical articles mostly published after the revival of interest in Fitzgerald following his death.

MOSELEY, EDWIN M. *F. Scott Fitzgerald* (Contemporary Writers in *Christian Perspective*). Grand Rapids, Mich.: William Eerdmans Publishing Co., 1967. Emphasizes the moral elements in Fitzgerald's writings, traceable in part to his Catholic background.

PEROSA, SERGIO. *The Art of F. Scott Fitzgerald.* Ann Arbor: University of Michigan Press, 1965. Translated from *L'Arte di F. Scott Fitzgerald.* Rome: Edizioni di Storia e Letteratura, 1961. Although written by an Italian scholar and carrying with it an academic flavor, it is still a good study.

PIPER, HENRY DAN, ed. *Fitzgerald's "The Great Gatsby": The Novel, The Critics, The Background.* New York: Scribner's, 1971. Brings between two covers the novel and source and critical materials bearing upon it.

SHAIN, CHARLES E. *F. Scott Fitzgerald.* Minneapolis: University of Minnesota Press, 1961. Brief, well-done guide in a series devoted to American writers.

SKLAR, ROBERT. *F. Scott Fitzgerald: The Last Laocoon.* New York: Oxford Press, 1968. Somewhat heavy book; still readable and provocative in its literary judgments.

STERN, MILTON R. *The Golden Moment: The Novels of F. Scott Fitzgerald.* Urbana: University of Illinois Press, 1969. An unfortunate style and much straining at critical insights mar this book.

4. Critical Essays

ASTRO, RICHARD. "*Vandover and the Brute* and *The Beautiful and Damned*: A Search for Thematic and Stylistic Reinterpretations," *Modern Fiction Studies*, XIV (Winter, 1968–69), 397–413. Brings out Fitzgerald's attraction to Frank Norris' works and traces parallels between the two novels.

ATKINSON, JENNIFER MCCABE. "Lost and Unpublished Stories by F. Scott Fitzgerald," *Fitzgerald/Hemingway Annual, 1971,* 32–63. Detailed account of nineteen stories located by a search through Harold Ober archives which were either never sold or published.

BABB, HOWARD S. "*The Great Gatsby* and the Grotesque," *Criticism,* V (Fall, 1963), 336–48. Argues that Fitzgerald's mingling of the "oddly humorous" and the "terrifying" is a chief source of the novel's power.

BARBOUR, BRIAN M. "*The Great Gatsby* and the American Past," *The Southern Review*, IX n.s. (Spring, 1973), 288–99. Relates conflicts in the novel to two versions of the American dream, the Emersonian and Franklinian.

BARRETT, WILLIAM. "Fitzgerald and America," *Partisan Review,* XVIII (May–June, 1951), 345–53. Review-essay of Mizener's biography. Fitzgerald's life is seen as "part of the American's emotional innocence before life."

BEWLEY, MARIUS. "Scott Fitzgerald and the Collapse of the American Dream," *The Eccentric Design: Form in the Classic American Novel.* New York: Columbia University Press, 1959. Penetrating discussion, particularly of "The Diamond as Big as the Ritz" and its relation to *The Great Gatsby* and to American myth.

BICKNELL, JOHN W. "The Waste Land of F. Scott Fitzgerald," *Virginia Quarterly Review*, XXX (Autumn, 1954), 556–72. Develops

Fitzgerald's use of the "wasteland" theme which appears most openly in *The Great Gatsby*.

BISHOP, JOHN PEALE. "The Missing All," *Virginia Quarterly Review*, XIII (Winter, 1937), 107–21. An assessment of Fitzgerald in relation to other writers of the 1920's, particularly Hemingway.

BRYER, JACKSON R. "F. Scott Fitzgerald and the State of American Letters in 1921," *Modern Fiction Studies*, XII (Summer, 1966), 265–67. Reprints a letter from Fitzgerald to Thomas Boyd assessing the contemporary literary scene.

————. "A Psychiatrist Reviews *Tender Is the Night*," *Literature and Psychology*, XVI (1966), 198–99. Affirmative assessment of Fitzgerald's psychological acuteness presumably by a psychiatrist writing in *Journal of Nervous and Mental Diseases* in 1935.

BURLINGAME, ROGER. *Of Making Many Books*. New York: Scribner's, 1946. Contains a number of interesting items involving correspondence with Fitzgerald during the publishing of his books.

CARDWELL, GUY A. "The Lyric World of Scott Fitzgerald," *Virginia Quarterly Review*, XXXVIII (Spring, 1962), 299–323. "The authentic marvel of Fitzgerald as a novelist is that sensitivity and lyric expressiveness can do so much."

CARLISLE, E. FRED. "The Triple Vision of Nick Carraway," *Modern Fiction Studies*, XI (Winter, 1965–66), 351–60. Sophisticated defense of the multiple perspectives of the narrator in *The Great Gatsby*.

COLEMAN, THOMAS C. "Nicole Warren Diver and Scott Fitzgerald: The Girl and the Egoist," *Studies in the Novel*, III (Spring, 1971), 34–43. Seeks to correct other critics' neglect of Fitzgerald's "basic misogyny." Romantic love of women will not satisfy a man's sense of romantic wonder.

COWLEY, MALCOLM. "Fitzgerald: The Double Man," *Saturday Review*, XXXIV (February 24, 1951), 9, 10, 42–44. Excellent statement about Fitzgerald's strength residing in his double nature or double vision. Other Cowley essays, equally valuable, are to be found in Kazin's collection and as introductions to *The Stories of F. Scott Fitzgerald* and *Three Novels of F. Scott Fitzgerald*.

DOHERTY, WILLIAM E. "*Tender Is the Night* and the 'Ode to a Nightingale.'" In Reck, Rima Drell, ed., *Explorations of Literature*. Baton Rouge: Louisiana State University Press, 1966, pp. 100–14. Closely argued essay on influence of Keats' poem on the writing of this novel.

DOS PASSOS, JOHN. "Fitzgerald and the Press," *New Republic*, CIV (February 17, 1941), 213. Short lead piece for a group of five essays as tributes to Fitzgerald following his recent death.

DOYNO, VICTOR. "Patterns in *The Great Gatsby*," *Modern Fiction Studies*, XII (Winter, 1966), 415–26. Examines the novel in terms of Fitzgerald's announced intent to make it "simple & intricately patterned."

DYSON, A. E. "*The Great Gatsby*: Thirty-Six Years After," *Modern Fiction Studies*, VII (Spring, 1961), 37–48. Excellent essay by an English critic which sets aside the novel's American roots and relates it to "the tragic predicament of humanity as a whole."

EBLE, KENNETH E. "The Craft of Revision: *The Great Gatsby*," *American Literature*, XXVI (November, 1964), 315–26. The first essay to examine closely the original manuscript of the novel and to discuss the many way in which Fitzgerald brought the novel to its ultimate shape.

————. "*The Great Gatsby*," *College Literature*, I, 1 (Winter, 1974), 34–47. Discusses the claims that can be made for *Gatsby* as a great novel if not *the* great American novel.

FORREY, ROBERT. "Negroes in the Fiction of F. Scott Fitzgerald," *Phylon*, XXVIII (1967), 293–98. Sheds light on how Fitzgerald was aware of and shared the social perceptions of his time.

FRASER, JOHN. "Dust and Dreams in *The Great Gatsby*," *Journal of English Literary History*, XXXII (1965), 554–64. Competent analysis of main themes in the novel.

FRIEDRICH, OTTO. "F. Scott Fitzgerald: Money, Money, Money," *American Scholar*, XXIX (Summer, 1960), 392–405. Valuable reassessment of Fitzgerald's reputation and worth. Praises *The Great Gatsby* and *Tender Is the Night* as great works; dismisses earlier novels.

FROHOCK, W. M. "Morals, Manners, and Scott Fitzgerald," *Southwest Review*, XL (Summer, 1955), 220–28. Argues that Fitzgerald deals essentially with manners; "felt life is the substance of the novel of manners."

FUSSELL, EDWIN. "Fitzgerald's Brave New World," *English Literary History*, XIX (December, 1952), 291–306. One of the first essays to emphasize Fitzgerald's work as "the tale of the romantic imagination in the United States ... the human imagination in the New World."

GEISMAR, MAXWELL. "F. Scott Fitzgerald: Orestes at the Ritz," *The Last of the Provincials: The American Novel, 1915–1925*. Boston: Houghton Mifflin, 1943. Extensive treatment of Fitzgerald's work in relation to the development of the modern American novel.

GILES, BARBARA. "The Dream of F. Scott Fitzgerald," *Mainstream*, X (March, 1957), 1–12. Far-left view of Fitzgerald which is more discerning than might be expected.

G[INGRICH], A[RNOLD]. "Publisher's Page—Will the Real Scott Fitzgerald Please Stand Up and Be Counted?" *Esquire* (December, 1964), pp. 8, 10, 12, 16.

————. "Scott, Ernest and Whoever," *Esquire* (December, 1966), pp. 186–89, 322–25.

Two excellent reminiscences by the long-time editor of *Esquire* who knew and championed both Fitzgerald and Hemingway. Fitzgerald's "big trouble was that he was a perfectionist in his living as much as in his writing."

GINDIN, JAMES. "Gods and Fathers in F. Scott Fitzgerald's Novels," *Modern Language Quarterly*, XXX (March, 1969), 64–85. Searching examination of Fitzgerald's moralism as it manifests itself and changes through all the novels.

GOODWIN, DONALD W. "The Alcoholism of F. Scott Fitzgerald," *Journal of the American Medical Association*, CCXII (April 6, 1970), 86–90. Physician examines the possible nature and causes of Fitzgerald's alcoholism and discusses alcoholism in relation to other writers as well. Reprints Fitzgerald's account to an American psychiatrist of a revealing dream about his mother.

GUERIN, WILFRED L. "Christian Myth and Naturalistic Deity: *The Great Gatsby*," *Renascence*, XIV, 2 (Winter, 1961), 80–89. Points the way to emphasizing the use of myth in this novel and in Fitzgerald's work. Focuses on the contrast between the Christian myth of the grail and the naturalistic deity.

HEARNE, LAURA GUTHRIE. "A Summer with F. Scott Fitzgerald," *Esquire* (December, 1964), pp. 160–65, 232, 236–37, 240, 242, 246, 250, 252, 254–58, 260. Reminiscence from the diary of the woman who was his secretary during the summer of 1935 in Asheville, North Carolina.

HUNT, JAN and JOHN M. SUAREZ. "The Evasion of Adult Love in Fitzgerald's Fiction," *The Centennial Review*, XVII, 2 (Spring, 1973), 152–69. Proceeding from a too firmly asserted understanding of neuroses, this article does examine the neurotic basis for Fitzgerald's depiction of women in his fiction and Fitzgerald's contrary impulses toward women in his life.

JACOBSON, DAN. "F. Scott Fitzgerald," *Encounter*, XIV (June, 1960), 71–77. Informed British opinion of Fitzgerald and the importance of his work, occasioned by the publication of the Bodley Head Fitzgerald.

KORENMAN, JOAN S. " 'Only Her Hairdresser . . .': Another Look at Daisy Buchanan," *American Literature*, XL, 4 (January, 1975), 574–78. Interesting attempt to show that the confusion in *The Great Gatsby* over whether Daisy is dark or fair reflects Fitzgerald's own ambivalence to women.

KUEHL, JOHN. "Scott Fitzgerald's Reading," *The Princeton University Library Chronicle*, XXII (Winter, 1961), 58–89. Fullest study of the range and intensity of Fitzgerald's literary interests.

————. "Scott Fitzgerald's Critical Opinions," *Modern Fiction Studies*, VII (Spring, 1961), 3–18.

LANAHAN, FRANCES SCOTT FITZGERALD. "Princeton and My Father," *Princeton Alumni Weekly* (March 9, 1956), pp. 8–9.

LISCA, PETER. "Nick Caraway and the Imagery of Disorder," *Twentieth Century Literature*, XIII (April, 1967), 18–28. Attempts to correct previous critics' contradictory interpretations of Nick's function as narrator.

LONG, ROBERT E. "The Great Gatsby and the Tradition of Joseph Conrad," *Texas Studies in Literature and Language*, VIII (Summer and Fall, 1966), 257–76, 407–22. The most searching study of the most important literary influence on Fitzgerald's work.

LUBELL, ALBERT J. "The Fitzgerald Revival," *South Atlantic Quarterly*, LIV (January, 1955), 95–106. Energetic but not very informed attack on Fitzgerald's high reputation.

MCCALL, DAN E. " 'The Self-Same Song That Found a Path': Keats and *The Great Gatsby*," *American Literature*, XLII (January, 1971), 421–30. Detailed study of a vital influence on Fitzgerald's writing; stresses both writers' fascination with the ambivalence of beauty.

MALE, ROY R. " 'Babylon Revisited': A Story of the Exile's Return," *Studies in Short Fiction*, II (Spring, 1965), 270–77. Shows how this story might be usefully related to other fiction which uses the theme of the Exile's Return.

MILLGATE, MICHAEL. "Scott Fitzgerald as Social Novelist: Statement and Technique in *The Last Tycoon*," *English Studies*, XLIII (February, 1962), 29–34. One of the best discussions of this uncompleted novel; perceives it as potentially a social novel radically different from *The Great Gatsby*.

MIZENER, ARTHUR. The many articles written by this leading Fitzgerald scholar are not listed here, since much of the material published prior to 1951 found its way into the biography. Among later articles, "The F. Scott Fitzgerald Papers," *The Princeton University Library Chronicle*, XII (Summer, 1951), 190–95; the Introduction and Headnotes to *Afternoon of an Author* (Scribner's, 1958); "The Maturity of Scott Fitzgerald," *Sewanee Review*, LXVII (Autumn, 1959), 658–75, "Scott Fitzgerald and the Top Girl," *Atlantic Monthly*, CCVII (March, 1961), 56–60, and "The Voice of Scott Fitzgerald's Prose," *Essays and Studies*, XVI (1963), 56–67, are valuable additions.

Modern Fiction Studies, VII, 1 (Spring, 1961). Special Fitzgerald number. The articles in this issue vary widely in quality, but the checklist of Fitzgerald criticism is invaluable.

MOK, MICHEL. "The Other Side of Paradise," *New York Post*, September 25, 1936, pp. 1, 15. This article caused Fitzgerald much pain in its insensitive depiction of him as a sick, alcoholic has-been.

MORRIS, WRIGHT. "The Ability to Function: A Reappraisal of Fitzgerald and Hemingway," *New World Writing*, XIII (June, 1958), 34–43.

NASON, THELMA. "Afternoon (and Evening) of an Author," *Johns Hopkins Magazine*, XXI (February, 1970), 2–15.

ORNSTEIN, ROBERT. "Scott Fitzgerald's Fable of East and West," *College English*, XVIII (December, 1956), 139–43. Excellent study of Fitzgerald's romantic vision in relation to the American West.

PARKER, DAVID. "*The Great Gatsby*: Two Versions of the Hero," *English Studies*, LIV, 1 (February, 1973), 37–51. Examines this novel against the background of English literature and in relation to experience common to all Western nations.

PIPER, HENRY DAN. "Frank Norris and Scott Fitzgerald," *Huntington Library Quarterly*, XIX (August, 1956), 393–400. In addition to Piper's articles in *The Princeton University Library Chronicle*'s Fitzgerald issue (Summer, 1951), "Scott Fitzgerald's Prep-School Writing," *Chronicle*, XVII (Autumn, 1955), 1–10, is also valuable. Piper's book *F. Scott Fitzgerald: A Candid Portrait* was published by Holt, Rinehart & Winston in 1965.

POWERS, J. F. "Cross-Country—St. Paul, Home of the Saints," *Partisan Review*, XVI (July, 1949), 714–21. Useful introduction to the city of St. Paul with a brief discussion of some of the uses Fitzgerald made of the city in his fiction.

PRIGOZY, RUTH. "A Matter of Measurement: The Tangled Relationship between Fitzgerald and Hemingway," *Commonweal* (October 29, 1971), 103–109. Good bringing together of materials which bear upon this complex personal and literary relationship.

Princeton University Library Chronicle, The, XII (Summer, 1951). Fitzgerald issue. Contain's Piper's check list, Mizener's account of the Fitzgerald Papers in Princeton Library, and other valuable items. The issue is almost impossible to buy but is available in many libraries.

REES, JOHN O. "Fitzgerald's Pat Hobby Stories," *Colorado Quarterly*, XXIII, 4 (Spring, 1975), 412–21. Exposition of the seventeen stories done for *Esquire*, 1939–40.

RIDDEL, JOSEPH N. "F. Scott Fitzgerald, the Jamesian Inheritance, and the Morality of Fiction," *Modern Fiction Studies*, XI (Winter, 1965–66), 331–50. Looks at Fitzgerald's heroes as "artists in sensibility" who embody a Jamesian equation of moral intelligence with artistic perception.

RING, FRANCES KROLL. "My Boss, Scott Fitzgerald," *Los Angeles Magazine*, VII (January, 1964), 34–36.

ROBBINS, J. ALBERT. "Fitzgerald and the Simple Inarticulate Farmer," *Modern Fiction Studies*, VII (Winter, 1961–62), 365–69. Reprints and discusses a letter Fitzgerald wrote to Maxwell Perkins in ♦925, deploring current fiction which sentimentalizes the man of the soil.

ROSENFELD, PAUL. "F. Scott Fitzgerald." In *Men Seen*. New York: Dial Press, 1925, pp. 215–24. One of the earliest and best critical appraisals of Fitzgerald's talents.

ROSS, ALAN. "Rumble Among the Drums—F. Scott Fitzgerald (1896–1940) and the Jazz Age," *Horizon*, XVIII (December, 1948), 420–35. Favorable British review of Fitzgerald's work; places special emphasis on the insight to be gained from reading Fitzgerald's own comments on his work through his essays, notebooks, and letters.

SAMUELS, CHARLES THOMAS. "The Greatness of 'Gatsby,'" *Massachusetts Review*, VII (Autumn, 1966), 783–94. Very laudatory essay on the greatness of this novel: "its fundamental achievement is a triumph of language."

SCHORER, MARK. "Some Relationships: Gertrude Stein, Sherwood Anderson, F. Scott Fitzgerald, and Ernest Hemingway." In *The World We Imagine*. New York: Farrar, Straus & Giroux, 1968, pp. 299–382.

SCHULBERG, BUDD. "Old Scott: The Mask, the Myth, and the Man," *Esquire*, LV (January, 1961), 96–101. Affords insight into Fitzgerald through reminiscences of a writer who knew and worked with Fitzgerald during the last years of his life.

SPENCER, BENJAMIN T. "Fitzgerald and the American Ambivalence," *South Atlantic Quarterly*, LXVI (Summer, 1967), 367–81. Argues that Fitzgerald wrote with effective authority on the inception and decay of American promises of happiness, shifting his assessment according to his own experiences and moods.

STALLMAN, R. W. "Gatsby and the Hole in Time," "Conrad and *The Great Gatsby*," "By the Dawn's Early Light *Tender Is the Night*." In *The Houses That James Built and Other Literary Studies*. East Lansing: Michigan State University Press, 1961, pp. 131–72.

TANSELLE, G. THOMAS and JACKSON R. BRYER. "*The Great Gatsby*—A Study in Literary Reputation," *New Mexico Quarterly*, XXXIII (Winter, 1963–64), 409–25. Careful charting of initial reviews and later revivals of interest which illuminate both the growth in the reputation of the novel and the nature of criticism during a forty-year span.

TAYLOR, DWIGHT. "Scott Fitzgerald in Hollywood," *Harper's* (March, 1959), pp. 67–71. First-hand account of the incident which provided Fitzgerald with the story "Crazy Sunday"; also appears in Taylor's book, *Joy Ride*, Putnam's, 1957.

THURBER, JAMES. "'Scott in Thorns,'" *The Reporter* (April 17, 1951), pp. 35–38. Account of the one meeting Thurber had with

Fitzgerald in 1934, "a lot of drinking and riding around in cabs . . . until dawn."

TOMKINS, CALVIN. "Living Well Is the Best Revenge," *New Yorker,* (July 28, 1962), pp. 31–32, 34, 36, 38, 43–44, 46–47, 49–50, 52, 54, 56–59. Long profile of Gerald and Sara Murphy; later published in book form, New York: Viking, 1971.

TUTTLETON, JAMES V. "F. Scott Fitzgerald: The Romantic Tragedian as Moral Fabulist." In *The Novel of Manners in America.* Chapel Hill: University of North Carolina Press, 1972. Fine discussion of Fitzgerald's place as a novelist of manners.

VANDERBILT, KERMIT. "James, Fitzgerald, and the American Self-Image," *Massachusetts Review,* VI (Winter-Spring, 1965), 289–304. Explores the possibility that T. S. Eliot's favorable response to *The Great Gatsby* in 1925 recognized in Fitzgerald the moral historian and critic which American fiction had not possessed since Henry James.

WARREN, DALE. "(Signed) F. S. F.," *The Princeton University Library Chronicle,* XXV (Winter, 1964), 129–36.

WEST, REBECCA. *Ending in Earnest.* Garden City, N. Y.: Doubleday, Doran, 1931. One of the few mentions of Fitzgerald as a serious writer between 1927 and 1934.

WESTBROOK, J. S. "Nature and Optics in *The Great Gatsby,*" *American Literature,* XXXII (March, 1960), 78–84. Example of close textual study which reaches some sensible conclusions about Fitzgerald's visual imagery in *The Great Gatsby.*

WILSON, EDMUND. "A Weekend at Ellerslie," *The Shores of Light.* New York: Farrar, Straus, 1952. All of Wilson's essays about Fitzgerald are valuable. They are reprinted in his *The Shores of Light, A Literary Chronicle: 1920–1950,* in *Discordant Encounters,* in Kazin's collection of criticism, and in Hoffman's study of *The Great Gatsby.*

Index

Novels, important articles and short stories, and important fictional characters are indexed below; minor fiction and characters may be found under references to novels and to collections of short stories.